For Auntie Sandra and Uncle Jim, with love. – J.H.

*For all the questioners everywhere –
Keep Asking! – J.L.*

I thank everyone involved in the production of this book for this great experience, both working and learning, and to all who have supported my work since the beginning – A.D.

A TEMPLAR BOOK

First published in the UK in 2023 by Templar Books,
an imprint of Bonnier Books UK,
4th Floor, Victoria House,
Bloomsbury Square, London WC1B 4DA
Owned by Bonnier Books,
Sveavägen 56, Stockholm, Sweden
www.bonnierbooks.co.uk

Text copyright © 2023 by Joan Haig and Joan Lennon
Illustration copyright © 2023 by André Ducci
Design copyright © 2023 by Templar Books

1 3 5 7 9 10 8 6 4 2

All rights reserved

ISBN 978-1-80078-353-9

This book was typeset in Archer and Tomarik.
The illustrations were created digitally.

Edited by Carly Blake and Rachael Roberts
Designed by Jeni Child
Production by Neil Randles

Printed in Poland

MIX
Paper | Supporting
responsible forestry
FSC® C018236

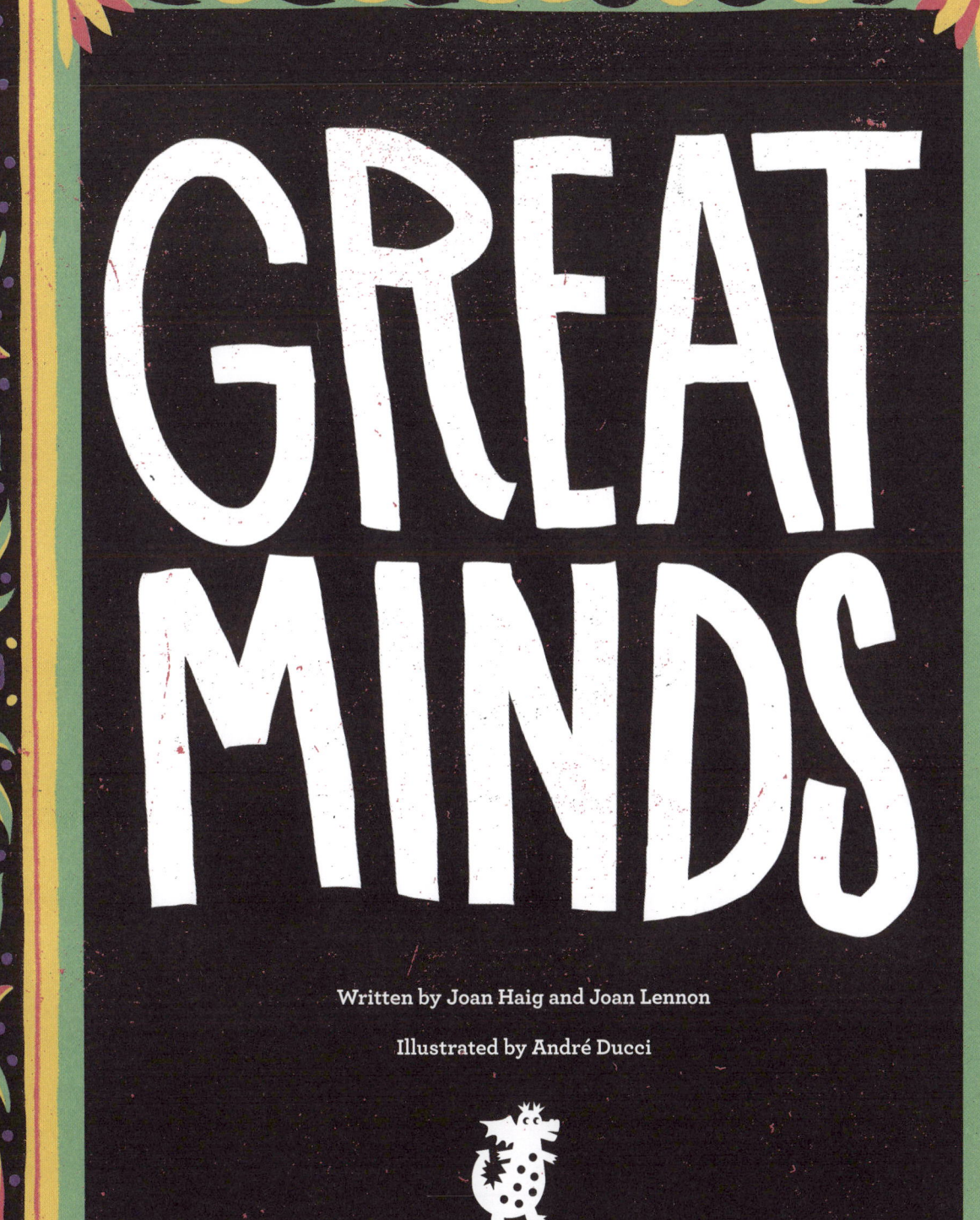

GREAT MINDS

Written by Joan Haig and Joan Lennon

Illustrated by André Ducci

templar
books

WHAT'S PHILOSOPHY FOR?

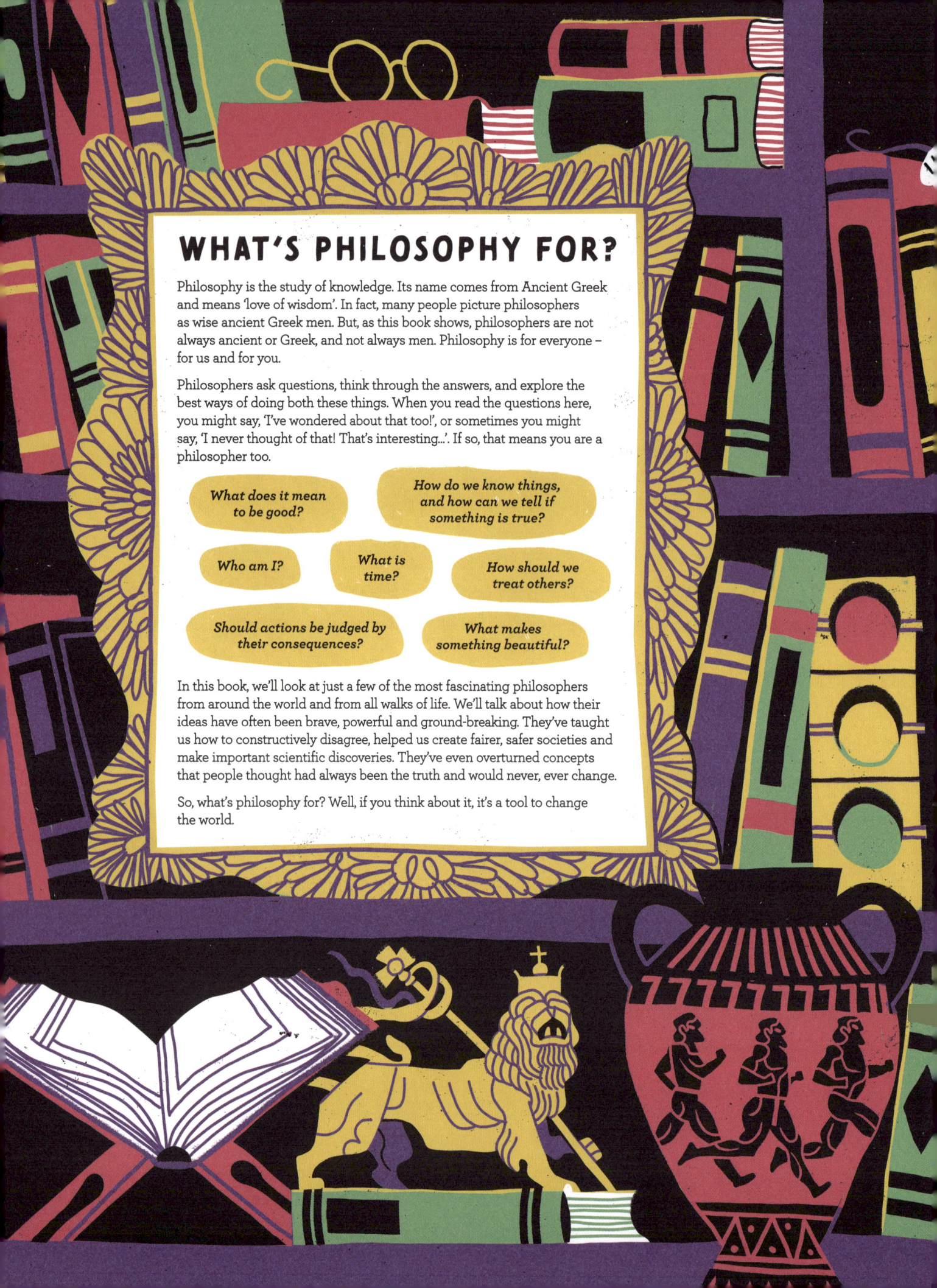

Philosophy is the study of knowledge. Its name comes from Ancient Greek and means 'love of wisdom'. In fact, many people picture philosophers as wise ancient Greek men. But, as this book shows, philosophers are not always ancient or Greek, and not always men. Philosophy is for everyone – for us and for you.

Philosophers ask questions, think through the answers, and explore the best ways of doing both these things. When you read the questions here, you might say, 'I've wondered about that too!', or sometimes you might say, 'I never thought of that! That's interesting...'. If so, that means you are a philosopher too.

- What does it mean to be good?
- How do we know things, and how can we tell if something is true?
- Who am I?
- What is time?
- How should we treat others?
- Should actions be judged by their consequences?
- What makes something beautiful?

In this book, we'll look at just a few of the most fascinating philosophers from around the world and from all walks of life. We'll talk about how their ideas have often been brave, powerful and ground-breaking. They've taught us how to constructively disagree, helped us create fairer, safer societies and make important scientific discoveries. They've even overturned concepts that people thought had always been the truth and would never, ever change.

So, what's philosophy for? Well, if you think about it, it's a tool to change the world.

ABOUT THE BOOK

This book is organised into chapters, each of which tells the story of a philosopher, a group of philosophers or a collective philosophy. It presents the historical time and place they are from, some of their questions, what led them to ask them, and what kinds of answers they came up with.

Key ideas from each thinker's philosophy have a heading with a special font (THIS ONE) and are written in *italics*.

If you get stuck on a difficult word or phrase, head to the glossary at the back of the book to find out what it means.

At the end of each chapter, we've highlighted some other philosophers you could find out about and the fascinating ideas they have to explore!

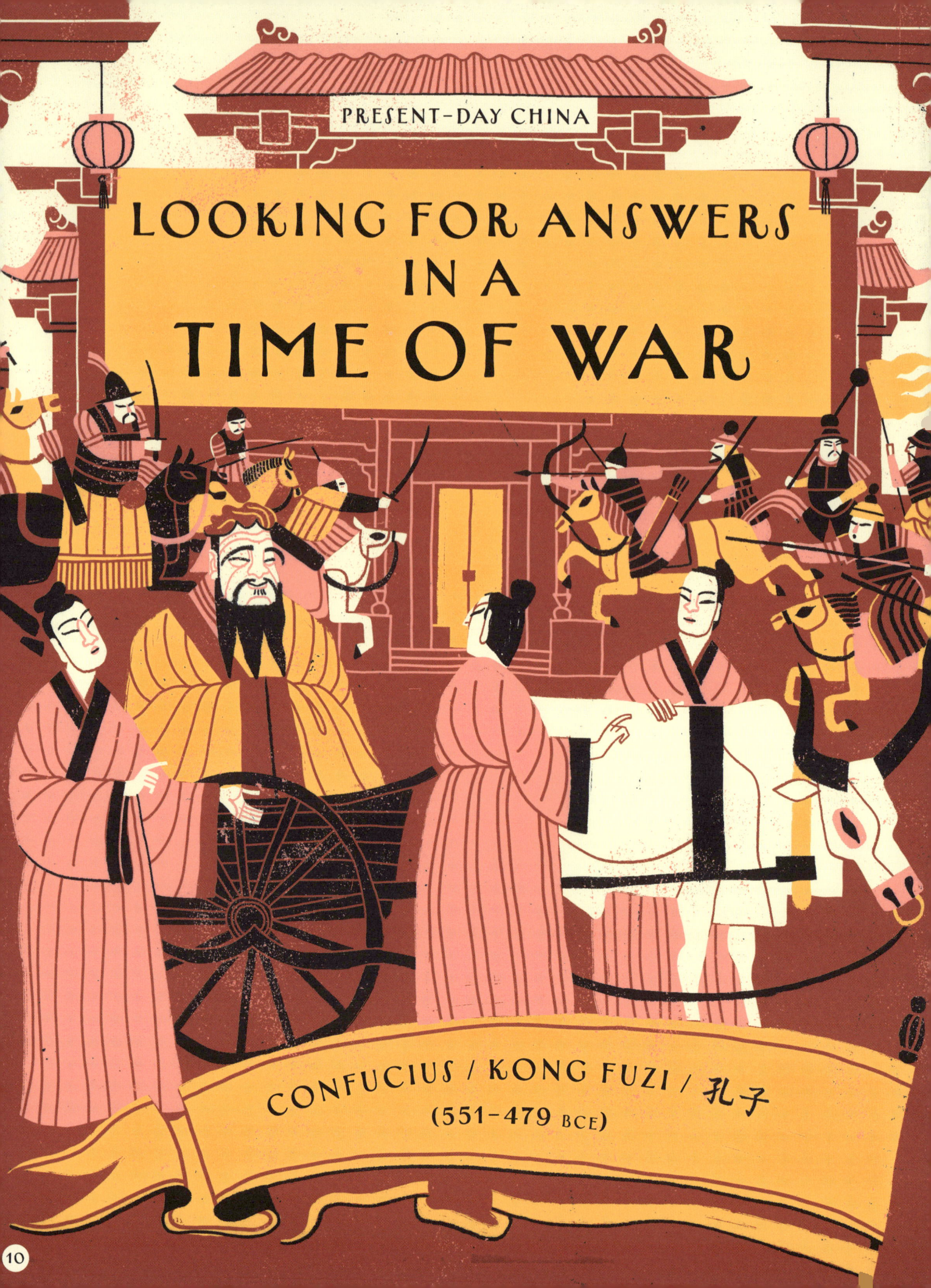

THINGS FALLING APART

For many years, the Zhou dynasty (about 1050–256 BCE) had been a time of peace and order, with the land's far-flung states all under the control of the central government. Music and literature flourished and there were clear ideas of how people should behave. By the time Confucius was born, however, things were breaking down. The states were at war with each other and the old ways were disappearing.

BORN INTO TROUBLED TIMES

Confucius's father was a soldier. He died when Confucius was three, leaving the young boy to be raised in poverty by his mother. In the social hierarchy of Confucius's time, he was considered *shi* – one class above common people. This meant he had access to education despite his poverty. After years of schooling, he worked his way up in the government, becoming an advisor to the local ruler. But unlike others in government, Confucius wanted to use his respected position to help others.

THE HUNDRED SCHOOLS OF THOUGHT

As the years of chaos dragged on, scholars and teachers struggled to make sense of what was happening around them.

 *Why is this happening?*

 *How can we make it stop?*

 *What does it mean to be good?*

With so many answers and solutions to these questions being considered, this time was later named the Hundred Schools of Thought. Like many of the other thinkers, Confucius looked to the past to find ways of creating a better future.

ON THE ROAD

Disappointed with the local ruler's leadership and refusal to follow his teachings, Confucius decided to leave his job. For the next 14 years, he and a group of his students travelled great distances through the war-torn countryside in search of a new ruler to guide in more honourable ways.

There were hardships and dangers, and at one point they nearly starved. But, as they walked, mile after mile, they talked and argued and asked many philosophical questions, testing and shaping Confucius's ideas as they went. In the end, they found no ruler willing to listen and Confucius returned home to continue teaching.

CONFUCIUS'S NEW NAME

Beginning in the 16th century, Jesuit priests were sent from Europe to learn about Chinese culture as a first step to converting the Chinese people to Christianity. They translated many Chinese texts into Latin, including a book of Confucius's sayings. Chinese names were also Latinised, so Kong Fuzi became Confucius.

CONFUCIUS THE TEACHER

In Confucius's time, people were ranked according to their class. Commoners – farmers, merchants and workers – were at the bottom and were expected to stay in these jobs. Next came different ranks of nobles, and at the top was the ruler.

Confucius thought that what made a person good was not the class they were born into, but their desire to learn. Many of Confucius's students came from lower classes. He believed if they were given access to education, they could gain the skills needed to work in the government and make society better for everyone.

THE DUKE OF ZHOU

Even though he lived long before Confucius was born, the Duke of Zhou (1042–1035 BCE) was Confucius's hero – a ruler who put the needs of the people first and was not corrupted by power. Confucius wanted to find a leader for his own time who he could encourage to be like the Duke of Zhou.

Junzi 俊子　Li 李　Ren 任

JUNZI, LI AND REN

Central to Confucius's philosophy were three key ideas: junzi, li and ren. The Duke of Zhou was an example of what Confucius called a junzi or good person – someone who led others by the example of their honourable actions and moral character.

For Confucius, some honourable actions were ones that followed the idea of li, which meant properly performing rituals. One such action was carefully observing traditional ceremonies at court. Li also applied to the way people behaved towards each other. In a family, this included how children should show respect to their parents and how parents should look after the needs of their children. In society, li was demonstrated when a person of lower status showed respect to someone higher, or when a high-status person used their power to look after people of lower status.

Finally, if li was goodness that could be seen on the outside in the honourable ways a junzi acted, then ren was goodness on the inside, reflected in a person's thoughts and character. Inner goodness gave a junzi the strength to be good to others.

Confucius believed that through education, people could learn how to practise li and build their ren so that they could become a junzi. Because of this, he saw education as a lifelong pursuit, a delight, a responsibility and the best way for his country to achieve stability and peace.

The early Zhou dynasty was a golden age to Confucius. He wanted to reintroduce their values to his own time to bring harmony back to society. He studied their literature, music and rituals and taught his students to do the same. He believed the answers to the troubles he saw all around him lay in this earlier time. Confucius wanted to pass on the truths of the past, rather than invent new ones.

IF EVERYBODY SAYS SO, IT *MUST* BE TRUE!

Confucius said he had to look at all sides of an idea to even begin to understand it. He would never accept things just because they were said to be true, and he encouraged his students to do the same. Confucius said that if everybody disliked a person, it was important to wonder why. Then after viewing all sides, you can make up your own mind. Similarly, if everybody liked a person, you should think about this just as closely. Can you think of something you have questioned that everyone else believed to be true?

WHAT DID CONFUCIUS REALLY SAY?

Today there are hundreds of popular sayings attributed to Confucius without any evidence that he ever said them. The closest thing we have to knowing what he really said can be found in *The Analects*. This work is a collection of conversations between Confucius and his students, written down over several centuries after his death.

2,500 YEARS LATER...

Before his death in 479 BCE, Confucius worried that he would be forgotten. Since then, however, his philosophy has had an enormous effect on the history and culture of East Asia. Today there are over 5 million people worldwide who describe themselves as Confucians. His ideas about respect for the past, responsibility for others, and the importance of education have a daily impact on their lives, and even after 2,500 years, his name has not been forgotten.

Mencius/ Mengzi (c.372–289 BCE)
Sometimes referred to as 'the Second Sage', Mencius was an advocate of Confucianism in China, bringing his interpretation of Confucius's ideas to prominence.

Voltaire (1694–1778)
A French philosopher who admired Confucian ideas brought back by the Jesuits. He saw Confucianism as the perfect combination of tolerance and reason, and he kept a picture of Confucius on his library wall.

Peng Chun Chang (1892–1957)
A Chinese diplomat and philosopher who was instrumental in instilling Confucian principles in the Universal Declaration of Human Rights.

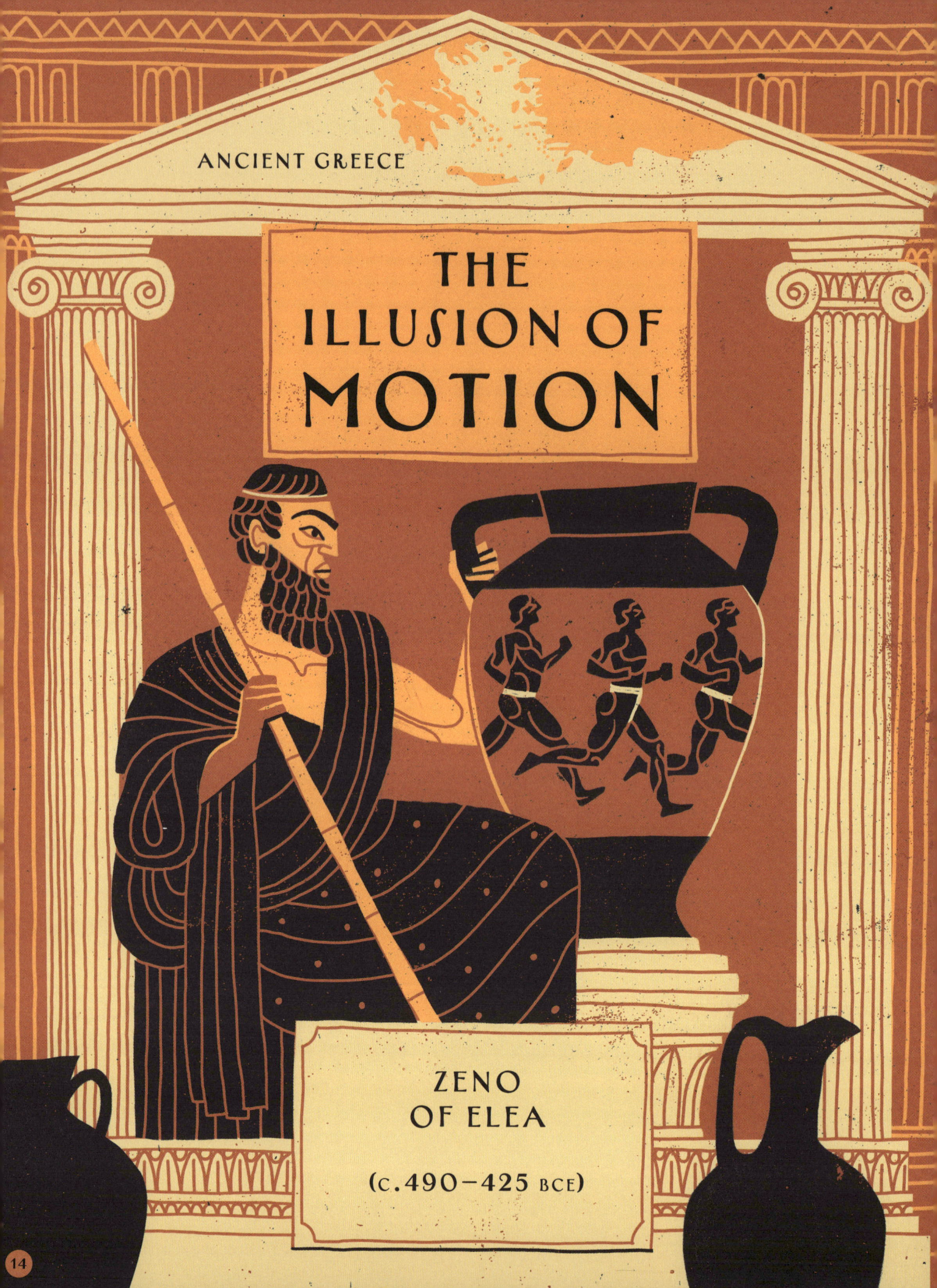

THE MYSTERIOUS PHILOSOPHER

Zeno was born around 490 BCE in Elea, a city in Magna Graecia — a Greek-speaking area of what is now southern Italy. We don't know much about his life because only fragments of his own writing exist and surviving details about him are sparse. But we do know that his ideas shook the world of philosophy.

THE ELEATIC SCHOOL

Elea was also home to one of the most influential philosophers of the time, a man called Parmenides. Born c.515 BCE, many accounts of Parmenides suggest he was an important person in the city, even helping to write its laws. His only philosophical writing was a poem that was 800 verses long! In it, he showed that reason and experience often produce different understandings of the world around us. He is considered the founder (in Europe) of ontology – the study of the nature of being.

MONISM

Philosophers of the Eleatic School believed in the theory of monism.

Monism says that the world around us must be made of singular things, and if something exists in reality – if it is real – then it cannot be divided into smaller things. This is because each of those things could then be divided into even smaller things, and so on until the initial thing can no longer be said to exist.

Many people thought this idea was rather strange, and Zeno's own thoughts developed while defending some of his teacher's ideas.

Zeno was a close companion and student of Parmenides, and one of the philosophers of the Eleatic School. This was not a 'school' in the way we think of them, with classrooms and teachers and dinner halls. Instead, 'school' meant those who followed Parmenides's beliefs and particular way of thinking – his 'school of thought'.

PRESOCRATIC PHILOSOPHY

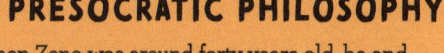

When Zeno was around forty years old, he and Parmenides travelled to the Greek city of Athens. There they met a young man called Socrates, who would later become one of the greatest and most famous thinkers of all time.

Unlike Zeno, Socrates was branching away from asking questions about existence and reality. He and the philosophers that followed him shifted their focus towards another type of philosophy called ethics. Zeno's work is referred to as Presocratic – that is, philosophy that came before Socrates. Hardly any of the Presocratic philosophers' original work survived, so most of what we know about their ideas comes from reports from later generations of Greek scholars and writers.

THE PARADOXES

Zeno is most known for his brain-bending paradoxes, some of which puzzled philosophers and mathematicians for hundreds of years. Although records suggest that he created over 40 paradoxes, only 10 are known today.

So, what exactly is a 'paradox'?

A paradox is something that seems both true and untrue at the same time, like a statement that contradicts itself or goes against common sense, or a problem that seems impossible to solve.

Everything I say is a lie!

What came first, the chicken or the egg?

The word 'paradox' comes from Ancient Greek *paradoxos*. *Para* means 'against' and *doxa* means 'belief'. Zeno challenged everyday thinking and people's beliefs about the world around them. He did so by devising these ingenious paradoxes to question the nature of objects, motion and place.

THE ILLUSION OF MOTION

Zeno liked to challenge how people thought about motion – how things move. He created scenarios using characters from Greek mythology to help people picture the problems he was describing.

ATALANTA AND THE STADIUM

In Greek mythology, Atalanta was a huntress and runner who was unbeatable by any other person in a fair sprint. But Zeno claimed that it was impossible for Atalanta, or anyone else for that matter, to begin – never mind to win – a race. Why is that?

Well, Zeno said that if Atalanta wanted to run from the start to the finish line of a race, she would first have to travel half the way to the finish line. Then to reach the halfway point, Atalanta first must travel half the distance to that point (that is, a quarter of the way to the finish line). To reach there, she must first travel half of that distance, and so on.

However small the distance becomes, Atalanta would always need to get halfway there first. Therefore, Zeno said, it would be impossible for her to get anywhere.

ACHILLES AND THE TORTOISE

Another paradox featured Achilles, the greatest warrior in Greek mythology. Imagine Achilles is racing against a tortoise. Since the tortoise is a slow creature, Achilles gives it a head start. Can Achilles win the race?

Zeno said no, Achilles would never be able to overtake the tortoise! No matter how small the tortoise's head start, Achilles would always have to reach the point where the tortoise had begun first. By then, the tortoise would have crept ahead and Achilles would have to reach the tortoise's new position, by which time it would have crept ahead some more. Therefore, Achilles would never be able to advance past the tortoise and win the race.

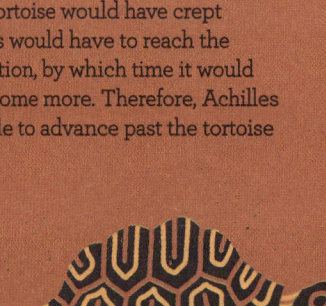

THE ARROW

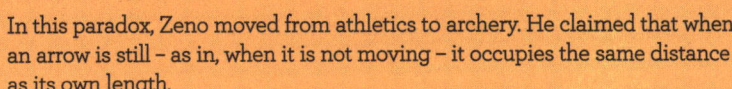

In this paradox, Zeno moved from athletics to archery. He claimed that when an arrow is still – as in, when it is not moving – it occupies the same distance as its own length.

Now, imagine an arrow in flight. At every given moment of the arrow's flight, the arrow will be occupying a space the same distance as its own length. Therefore, a flying arrow is never moving! But how could that be?

Well, it's just not true! Of course, we know that Atalanta could start running a race, that Achilles could overtake the tortoise and that a flying arrow is moving. But what Zeno's paradoxes show us is that while we know something to be true, we may not know how or why it is true. We can never simplistically trust our perceptions about the physical world around us.

REDUCTIO AD ABSURDUM!

Zeno's approach is often referred to as an example of *reductio ad absurdum* – which sounds like a wizard's spell but is actually Latin for 'reduction to absurdity'. In other words, philosophers sometimes think of extreme (and absurd) examples to prove or test their ideas.

INFINITELY PUZZLING

For centuries, some of the greatest thinkers tried to solve Zeno's puzzles. A breakthrough came when mathematician and physicist Isaac Newton set out his laws of physics, helping us understand motion. He and others developed a branch of mathematics called calculus.

Zeno treated time and distance as separate things that can be infinitely divided into smaller parts. But calculus teaches us that there are relationships between time and distance, and also speed and direction. These relationships are key to understanding how things move. For example, if Achilles is faster than the tortoise, the time it takes him to cover a certain distance is shorter. If the racetrack is long enough, Achilles will overtake the tortoise.

However, even if we know more now than 2,500 years ago, it appears there is no limit to our interest in Zeno's puzzles, ideas and the theories they set in motion.

Plutarch (c.50–120 CE)
This Greek philosopher questioned the nature of reality. In his 'Ship of Theseus' paradox he asks if, over time, a ship is repaired and its parts replaced so many times that none of the original pieces remain, is it the same ship?

al-Ghazali (1059–1111)
A Persian thinker who said that Earth orbits around the Sun thirteen times more often than Jupiter. And in an infinite universe, Earth and Jupiter would rotate the same number of times. Puzzling!

Bertrand Russell (1872–1970)
This British mathematician created the 'Barber Paradox'. A barber works in a village where everyone is clean shaven. The barber shaves only those who do not shave themselves. Who shaves the barber?

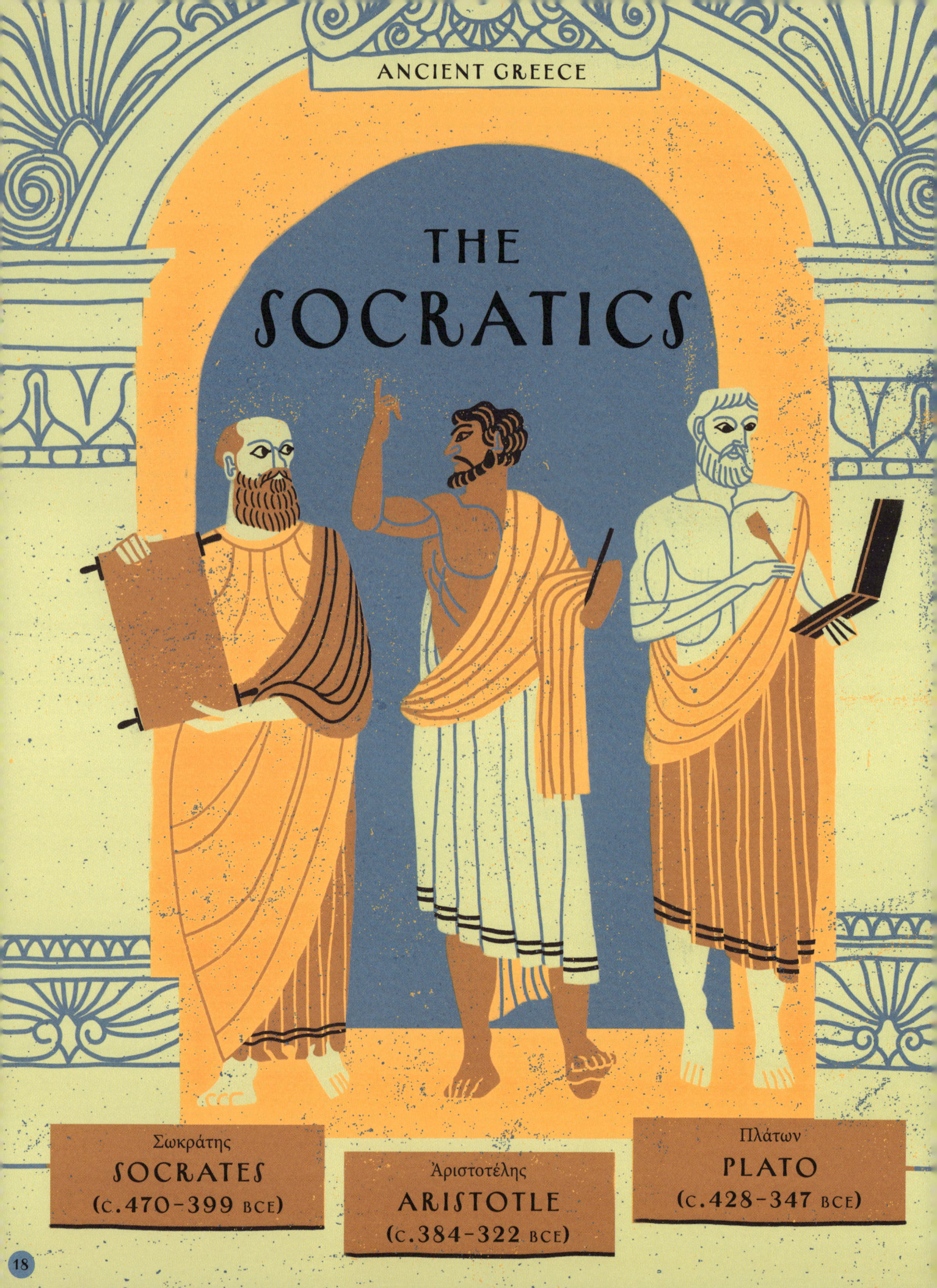

THREE DEFINING THINKERS

The Socratic philosophers were three big thinkers in ancient Greece. There was Socrates himself, his student Plato and Plato's student, Aristotle. Their fascinating ideas shaped and were shaped by the ancient Greek world, and they remain important figures in philosophical thought today.

Socrates Plato Aristotle

THE GOLDEN AGE OF ATHENS

Athens, where Socrates was born and lived, had emerged victorious from the Persian Wars (499-449 BCE), and the 'golden age' that followed saw the city flourish under the mighty general and democrat Pericles. Athens' newfound wealth and power was reflected in the building of temples such as the Parthenon, great statues, beautiful gardens and theatres. Citizens of Athens began to value beauty, high culture and intellectual thought.

SOCRATES' HUMBLE BEGINNINGS

Socrates did not come from a wealthy family, but he gained a reputation among important people in the city for his bravery as a soldier and for his unusual ideas. Less interested in beauty for its own sake, he wanted to understand truth and ethics and how to live a morally 'good' life.

THE ORACLE AT DELPHI

Socrates' friend Chaerephon went on a journey to visit the oracle at Delphi. According to the oracle, no one living was wiser than Socrates. This revelation surprised Socrates, who felt he knew so little, so he set out on a quest to become wise.

THE SOCRATIC METHOD

Socrates came up with a unique approach to becoming wiser. He wandered the city asking all kinds of people different questions.

When people answered, he would ask more questions and challenge their answers until either they reached a definitive answer or, more commonly, a state of confusion and uncertainty called aporia. We call this the Socratic method or Socratic dialectic.

KNOWING NOTHING

Socrates saw *aporia* as the first step towards learning. He encouraged people to doubt what they thought they knew, and to begin to think for themselves rather than accept wisdom they had been told. In his wanderings and teachings he therefore exposed false knowledge.

All I know is that I know nothing!

CAN A PERSON DO WRONG WILLINGLY?

Socrates believed that it is impossible for someone to do wrong willingly, and therefore wrongful acts come only from ignorance. If a person knows the right thing to do, will they always do it?

WHICH SOCRATES?

In philosophy, Socrates was actually two different people. One was a real person – Socrates the philosopher. The other was made up! The real Socrates never wrote things down, so what we know about him comes from written accounts, mostly by Plato. As well as writing about the real Socrates, Plato wrote his own ideas as dialogues with an imaginary character also called Socrates. How confusing!

DEATH BY POISON

The Golden Age of Athens wouldn't last. Tension with Sparta and its league of city-states was rising, eventually leading to all-out war. Amid this unrest, Socrates' constant questioning undermined and annoyed political decision-makers and he was labelled a dangerous influence.

In 399 BCE, Socrates was charged with impiety (going against the gods) and 'corrupting the youth' by inciting them to challenge authority. A jury found him guilty and sentenced him to death by poison. Socrates was imprisoned in a cave for thirty days and died by drinking brewed hemlock.

PLATO'S NEW START

Plato was born around 428 BCE into a rich, aristocratic family. He was about 20 years old when he met Socrates and he spent the following decade learning from him.

Plato was so devastated by the death of his teacher that he left Athens. He travelled to a place called Megara, and then to Egypt, Sicily and other parts of ancient Greece.

After returning from his travels, Plato began to write his own ideas and the ideas of Socrates. He also set up his own school of higher thought – the first of its kind in Europe. It was built in 380 BCE outside the city walls in an area called the *Akadēmeia*, or 'the Academy', and it remained open for 800 years.

THE THEORY OF FORMS

Plato's best-known philosophy is his theory of forms. For Plato, a form is the true version or idea of a thing, and the things that we see in the world around us are merely imitations of their ideal form.

For example, a potter will never be able to make a plate that is perfectly round, but a regular, geometric circle proves perfect roundness exists. Indeed, the potter aspires to this form when making a plate.

WHAT IS A CHAIR?

Here is another example. Picture a chair. Now look at these chairs:

None of these chairs are the same, and none probably match the chair that you pictured. But we probably agree that they are all chairs.

According to Plato's theory, this is because there exists an idea of a chair that is totally separate from what a chair might actually look like. This idea of a chair is its true form.

TWO REALMS

So, where do these forms exist? Plato said that the forms exist in an ideal world called the Realm of Being. This ideal world must exist, he claimed, because if there is such a thing as true knowledge then it must be fixed and certain – true now, true forever, true everywhere and for everyone.

In contrast, the natural world of our day-to-day lives is uncertain, always changing and contains only imperfect versions of the forms. He called this the Realm of Becoming. Within this realm, our senses constantly deceive us into thinking things are true when they are not.

THE ALLEGORY OF THE CAVE

To demonstrate how his theories worked together, Plato told this story.

There was once a cave where prisoners were held. They were chained up and made to face the cave's back wall. Behind them, a fire was burning and behind that, a tunnel led to the bright world outside.

Day and night, guards paced between the captives and the fire. They held up puppets that cast shadows of birds and animals and trees on the wall of the cave, and these shadows were all the prisoners could see.

One day, a prisoner escaped! In seeing the fire, he understood that what he and the others saw were only shadows of puppets. Then when he went out through the tunnel into the bright world, he understood that even the puppets were not the true forms.

WHAT'S PHILOSOPHY FOR?

Plato believed that part of a philosopher's job was to help people find the truth beyond the sensory world. Where do you think 'truth' exists? Is there a such a thing as an ideal world?

ARISTOTLE 'THE MIND'

Aristotle was born around 384 BCE in Stagira, in the Kingdom of Macedonia. As a teen, he moved to Athens and began learning at Plato's Academy where he spent the next 20 years.

Plato called him 'The Mind' because of his impressive knowledge and ability to think analytically. He asked many questions and contributed his knowledge in almost all disciplines, including arithmetic, art, astronomy, geography, literature, meteorology (the science of weather), politics, psychology and, of course, philosophy.

FROM STUDENT TO TUTOR

When Plato died in 347 BCE, Aristotle took his mentor's lead and left the Academy to travel. In 343 BCE, he went back to Macedonia on the invitation of King Philip to tutor his son, Alexander. Aristotle's pupil went on to become Alexander the Great, one of the world's greatest military generals.

On returning to Athens in 335 BCE, he set up his own school, the Lyceum, in a covered walkway of a gymnasium building. Here he would walk with students and deliver long lectures. Aristotle taught there for over a decade.

LOST MANUSCRIPTS AND FOUND DIALOGUES

Most of Aristotle's original published work was lost. However, his early dialogues – written in the style of his teacher, Plato – were inherited and passed on from scholar to scholar over generations, and stored in a cellar where they were nibbled by moths, mice and mould. In the year 1 BCE, his dialogues ended up in Rome where they were thankfully rescued by a philosopher called Andronicus of Rhodes.

OBSERVING THE NATURAL WORLD

Aristotle often identified shared features called properties that could help sort things into groups, like types of plants or animals. In fact, he is seen as the inventor of biology because he wrote the earliest known classification of animals. He observed animals to understand their behaviour and dissected them to learn about their anatomy.

Aristotle's philosophy is based on collecting, observing, recording and classifying natural phenomena.

THE FOUR CAUSES

According to Aristotle, classifying things helps us understand them. In order to do this adequately, Aristotle claimed that we need to ask four central questions:

What is it for?

What is it made of?

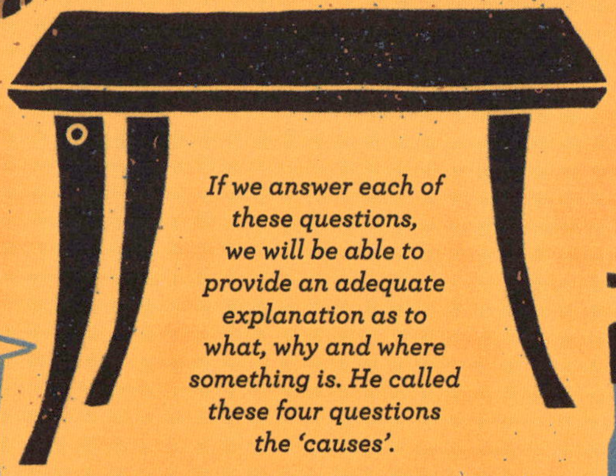

If we answer each of these questions, we will be able to provide an adequate explanation as to what, why and where something is. He called these four questions the 'causes'.

What is it?

What brought it about?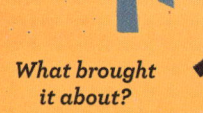

INVENTING LOGIC

Aristotle also believed that organising our ideas and the way we think would help us to think better – and therefore, to understand the world better. He established the science of reason, known as logic, and he categorised different types of logical argument. One logical argument he created is called a syllogism – a three-step argument that goes like this:

Every Greek is a human. Socrates is a Greek. Therefore, Socrates is a human.

Can you think of your own syllogism?

So, what makes a person virtuous?

Humans are unique for our ability to reason, and so a person who reasons well must be virtuous.

LIVING WELL

Like Socrates and Plato before him, Aristotle was interested in virtue and what it meant to live a 'good' life. He was particularly interested in *eudaemonia*, an ancient Greek idea of living well. Aristotle believed that every part of every living or human-made thing has a function, and that the value of the thing – what he considered its goodness or virtue – can be measured against how well it performs this function.

For example, a 'good' axe is one that is strong and sharp enough to cut wood but not too heavy to wield or swing.

THE GOLDEN MEAN

In theorising about reason and how to live a good life, Aristotle came up with the 'golden mean' – a perfect middle point between two extremes in which a person could find virtue.

In one example, he theorised that courage is the mean between cowardice (fearing too much) and rashness (fearing too little), and so courage is a virtuous, or good, trait.

THE LEGACY OF THE SOCRATICS

Aristotle's work was first translated into Arabic and Latin and then other languages, and spread across the world. Building on the work of Plato and Socrates before him, his thinking contributed vast amounts to knowledge and laid the foundations for modern scientific thought.

Antisthenes (c.446–366 BCE)
A pupil of Socrates and founder of 'Cynicism', whose followers believed that the way to lead a good life was to live simply and at one with nature.

Abū Naṣr al-Fārābī (c.870–950)
A bringer of Aristotle's ideas to the medieval Islamic world where he was one of its most influential thinkers.

John McDowell (1942–)
A South African philosopher whose early work included translations of Plato and whose later work focused on Aristotelian ethics.

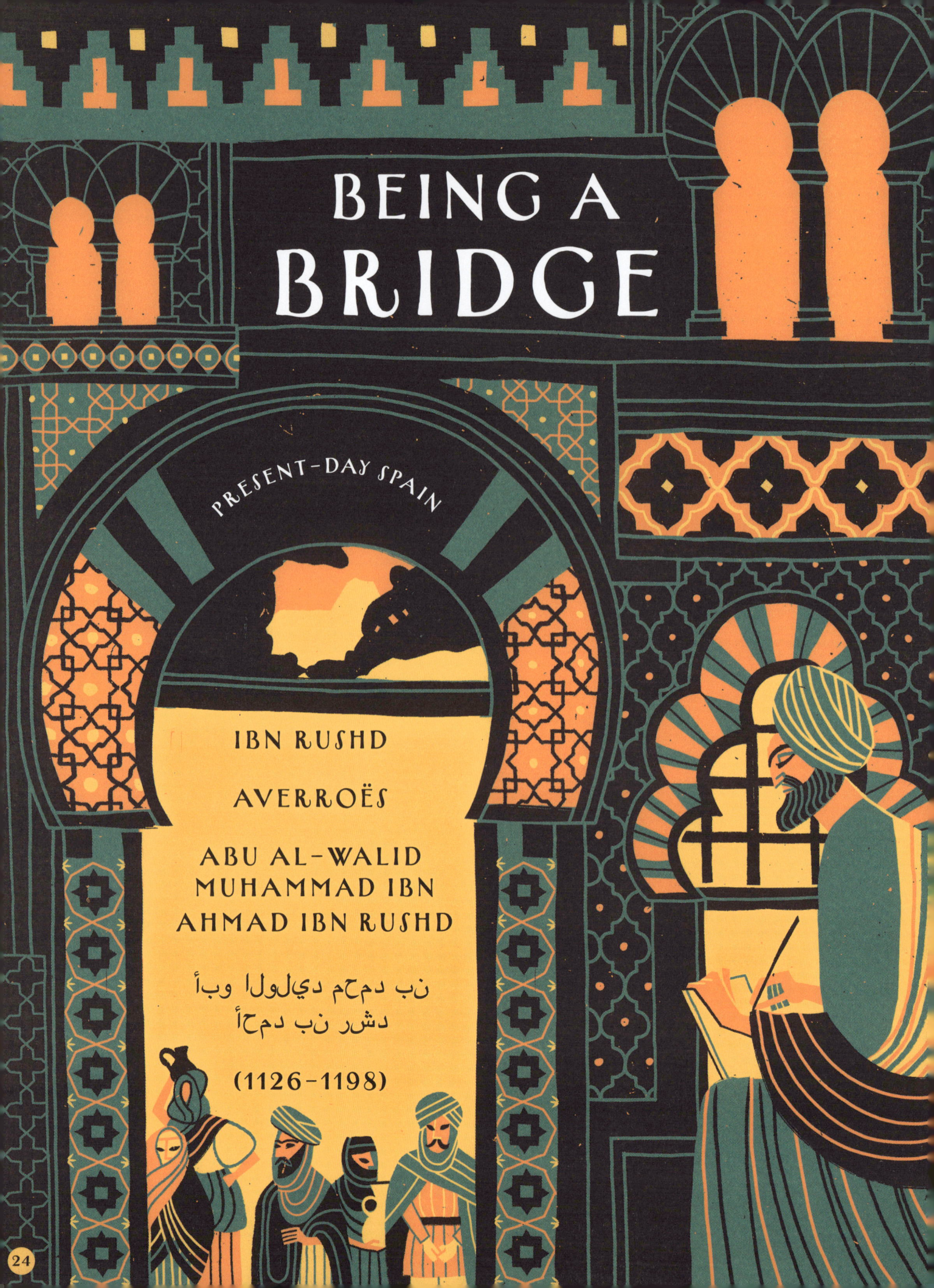

THE ISLAMIC GOLDEN AGE

The city of Córdoba was prospering in the 12th century. Minarets soared above the houses and the call to prayer echoed over the rooftops. Fountains sparkled in green gardens and traders with goods and travellers with stories from all over the world thronged the streets. The Iberian Peninsula (present-day Spain and Portugal) was in the midst of the Islamic Golden Age, which began in 711 CE and would last for almost 800 years. Music and art were celebrated, there were advances in science and medicine, and Muslims, Jews and Christians worked and lived together. This was the world Ibn Rushd was born into in 1126 CE.

EDUCATING THE CALIPH

Little is known about Ibn Rushd's early life except that he was well educated in Islamic law, theology and medicine. His grandfather and father were well-regarded judges in Córdoba, so it was no surprise when Ibn Rushd began to move in the highest circles of the court. His work as a judge and physician (a type of doctor) impressed the ruler, Caliph Abu Yaqub Yusuf. One day, the Caliph complained to Ibn Rushd that he had trouble understanding the writings of Aristotle and asked him to take on the task of explaining them.

THE WORK OF A LIFETIME

Ibn Rushd accepted the Caliph's challenge and the result was his most famous work, *The Commentaries*. For nearly 30 years, he read and re-read the Greek philosophers, comparing translations and making notes and observations. He worked to understand and clarify their ideas so that they could speak to his own time, becoming a bridge between the ancient Greek world and his Islamic present.

BEING A POLYMATH

Ibn Rushd wasn't only fascinated by philosophy. He studied many subjects, including medicine, anatomy, psychology, law, theology, music and astronomy, and he wrote about each of them. He was one of the first people to observe and describe dark circles on the Sun called sunspots, and he explained how strokes are caused by blood not getting to the brain. Ibn Rushd worked very hard, and it was said that he never missed a day writing. His contributions were so many that today there is a crater on the moon named after him.

IN DEFENCE OF PHILOSOPHY

Ibn Rushd valued what philosophy has to teach us. As he read and explained the ancient Greeks, he expanded on their ideas where he felt they could be improved. But his comments weren't limited to the writings of the distant past. The Persian religious scholar al-Ghazali (1058–1111 CE) wrote a book criticising philosophy called *The Incoherence of the Philosophers*. Ibn Rushd fought back with his work, *The Incoherence of the Incoherence*, passionately defending philosophy as an essential path to truth and understanding.

FIRE AND COTTON

Al-Ghazali said that when fire and cotton are brought together, the cotton burns because God wills it to. Ibn Rushd argued back that if fire is put to cotton, it will alight because of natural law – the rules that determine how the physical world works. He did, however, say that God created natural laws, and the more we use reason to understand them, the closer we can get to God's truth. Philosophy to Ibn Rushd was a way of using our God-given reasoning abilities, which in turn would strengthen our faith.

FICTION AND FACT

In another book, Ibn Rushd wrote that the Qur'an teaches us to look at the natural world using reason. At the same time, he noted there are passages in the Qur'an that deny what our reasoning has shown to be true. But how are we meant to understand this?

Ibn Rushd said that these passages are stories, not literal facts, and we should look for what these stories are trying to teach us. Do you know any stories that try to teach us a lesson? Do you think stories can tell truths? Or can only scientific, provable facts be true?

THE ABILITIES OF WOMEN

Some of Ibn Rushd's ideas were considered controversial. For example, he said women were just as capable as men of understanding truth. Muslim women at that time were expected only to be wives and mothers and were told to stay at home. Ibn Rushd argued women should not be prevented from taking part in the world or in philosophy.

IS PHILOSOPHY FOR EVERYBODY?

Despite arguing that women are as capable of thinking philosophically as men, Ibn Rushd was not convinced that everyone would understand philosophy and religion in the same way. For uneducated people at the time, he thought that philosophy was, in fact, a bad idea – it would confuse them and turn them away from believing in the Qur'an. Philosophy was only safe for educated men and women to study, as they would understand the important truths of both philosophy and faith.

BRIDGING THE PAST AND THE FUTURE

The Caliph's challenge to explain the words of Aristotle wouldn't only prove fruitful in Ibn Rushd's time. After his death, his work would ensure the ancient Greek philosophers were not forgotten, making Ibn Rushd a bridge between the past and the future.

DIVERGING LEGACIES

ISLAMIC THOUGHT

Towards the end of Ibn Rushd's life, stricter religious groups within Islam were gaining power and philosophy was treated with suspicion. As a result, at age 69, the philosopher was sent into exile. His writings were banned and his books were burned. Two years later, Ibn Rushd was pardoned, but he died not long after that. In the period that followed, Islamic interest in philosophy largely ended, but that wasn't the case elsewhere in the world...

JEWISH THOUGHT

Ibn Rushd's texts were translated from Arabic into Hebrew, and Jewish thinkers began to comment on his commentaries, discussing his ideas as well as Aristotle's. Ibn Rushd was seen as the authority on Greek philosophy, and Greek philosophy was seen as essential learning.

CHRISTIAN THOUGHT

Following Ibn Rushd's death, the first great European universities were established. There the study of philosophy and science began to flourish, and there was a rise in interest in the Greek philosophers whose work had been lost or ignored since the 6th century. It was Ibn Rushd's explanations of Aristotle and Plato translated into Latin that were primarily used. He became known by his Latinised name, Averroës, or simply as 'The Commentator'.

THE ARAB SPRING

In modern times, Ibn Rushd's philosophy was important to many who took part in the Arab Spring, a series of pro-democracy protests in the Middle East and North Africa between 2010 and 2013. Protestors saw him as speaking to them across the centuries, telling them of the ways reason and faith can combine to lead to truth.

Maimonides (1138–1204)
A Jewish philosopher who worked on reconciling Aristotle's ideas and the Torah, just as Ibn Rushd worked on harmonising Aristotle's ideas and the Qur'an.

Thomas Aquinas (1225–1274)
An Italian friar and philosopher who was influenced by Ibn Rushd. Aquinas respected Ibn Rushd as 'The Commentator' despite disagreeing with him on many issues.

Arab Renaissance (late 19th – early 20th century)
During this time, Ibn Rushd's ideas on reason and religion found a new audience in political and cultural debates in Egypt, Syria and beyond.

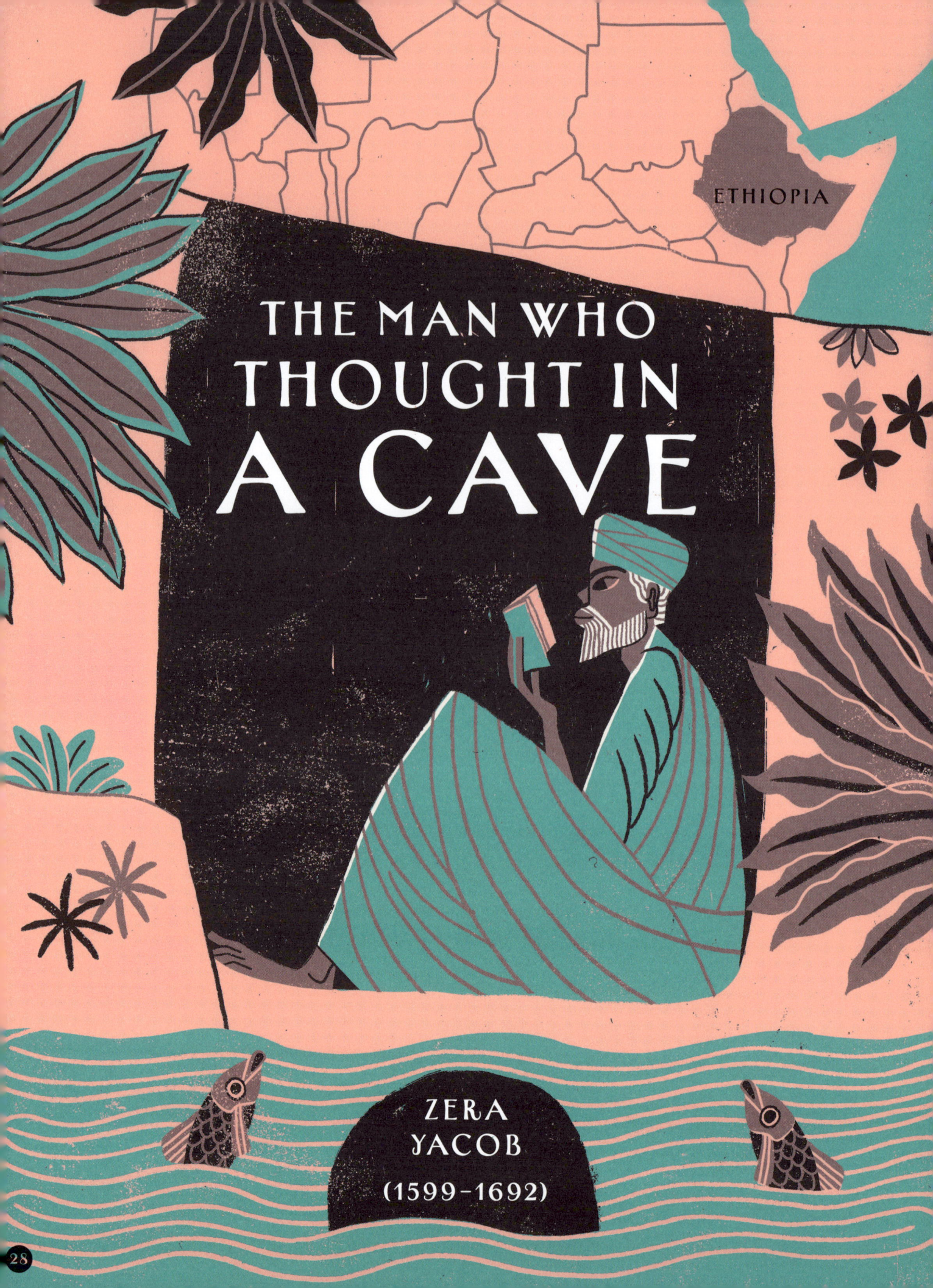

AN ANCIENT CHRISTIAN NATION

Ethiopia is one of the oldest Christian countries in the world. Since the early 4th century, the Ethiopian Orthodox Church was the nation's main religion, developing its own practices and beliefs that were ingrained in Ethiopian culture. Then, in the 16th century, a Muslim general from Somalia named Ahmed Grāñ invaded the country's highlands. After an unsuccessful attempt to fight him off, the Ethiopians asked for help from Portuguese soldiers. Jesuit priests soon followed, and after finding influence at court, they began their bid to become the nation's dominant religion.

A BOY FROM A FARM

Zera Yacob's father was an ordinary farmer, and the family was not well to do. But as a boy, Yacob excelled at school and his family were encouraged to send him to masters who taught advanced subjects like music, poetry and grammar. The first master teased Yacob for his coarse singing voice; so feeling dejected, he left to learn from someone else.

FALLING VICTIM TO RELIGIOUS CONFLICT

Over the next 14 years, Yacob studied ways of interpreting the Bible with different scholars. Across the country, the Jesuits were trying to replace the Ethiopian Orthodox Church with their own Roman Catholic Church, and the conflict between the two groups became ever more fierce. Yacob could see good and bad things in both faiths and refused to choose one over the other. He was denounced to King Susenyos, who had been converted by the Jesuits and persecuted any of his subjects who didn't follow suit. Yacob's life was suddenly in danger.

THE CAVE OF THOUGHTS

Yacob fled in the dead of night with some gold he had earned and just one book that contained the Psalms of David. He headed south, afraid of everyone he met, until one day, walking along the Tekezé River, he saw a lonely cave at the head of an uninhabited valley. This was to be his home for the next two years.

Yacob lived in isolation as a hermit, speaking to no one except on occasional trips to a nearby village to buy food. He spent his time thinking in the quiet of his cave, struggling with questions about his relationship with God and how to know what was true when there was so much disagreement in the world outside. He later said he came to understand more in his solitude than in all the years he had been at school.

A NEW LIFE

When Susenyos' reign ended in 1632, Yacob felt it was safe to leave his cave.

Unwilling to return to his old life, he settled instead in the town of Enfraz, where he made a copy of the Psalms of David for a rich merchant named Habtu. Others began to admire his handwriting and asked him to make more copies. Yacob had found a new way of life.

Habtu then asked Yacob to teach the subjects he had studied for many years to his two youngest sons, Walda Gabryel and Walda Heywat. Impressed with his teacher, Walda Heywat later asked Yacob to write down his ideas and tell the story of his life.

ZERA YACOB'S HATÄTA

In his cave, Yacob had thought long and hard about the questions that had troubled him in the outside world. These questions would later inspire him to write a book called *Hatäta*, meaning an investigation or inquiry in the Ethiopian language Ge'ez. The book tells how the events of his life led Yacob to his ideas, which he hoped would help others clarify their own thoughts.

THE FIRST QUESTION:
DOES GOD EXIST?

Seeing the different churches violently persecute each other, doing evil in God's name, Yacob wondered why God was allowing this. In a moment of great sadness, he even wondered if God existed. But if there was no God, how had the first thing been created? For creation to exist, Yacob argued there must be a creator.

Is it possible for something to come out of nothing?

THE SECOND QUESTION:
WHAT IS TRUTH?

Yacob thought God had created people imperfectly so that they could learn to become good by choosing what was true. But when studying with different scholars, he noticed each one was convinced that they knew the truth, despite it being different from what the next person said. Often their faith was based on what their parents had told them, which was what their parents had told them. Yacob asked if it is lazy to accept what you are told without using reason to question it?

How can we know if something's true? Can there be different truths?

THE THIRD QUESTION:
ARE WE ALL EQUAL?

Yacob reasoned that a loving God would not favour one group of people over another, but would see all his created children as equal. This went against the beliefs of the time that women were lesser than men, or that slavery, which was widely practised in Ethiopia, was acceptable.

Why do some people believe they are superior to others?

A FALSE INQUIRY?

Some people refused to accept that these ideas had come from Yacob because they believed only white Europeans could understand philosophy. We call this view Eurocentric.

I am Zera Yacob. I wrote the Hatäta in 1667.

I am Canadian scholar Claude Sumner. I analysed the Hatäta thoroughly and say of course it was written by Zera Yacob.

We are Ethiopian scholars Amsalu Alkilu and Almeyahu Moges. We say the Hatäta absolutely was written by someone educated in Ethiopian schools.

I am Giusto d'Urbino, a monk who discovered the Hatäta in 1852 while collecting manuscripts that were then given to the Paris Academy of Sciences.

I am Carlo Conti Rossini. I announced in 1920 that the Hatäta was a forgery because no Ethiopian could have written such a work. Giusto d'Urbino was its secret author.

SAME IDEAS, DIFFERENT PLACES

Yacob's ideas about thinking for yourself instead of believing others were similar to those of other philosophers of the European Enlightenment. But Yacob's ideas came to him independently. How could this be? Some philosophers have suggested there is a kind of collective knowledge that all people draw on. Another thought is that ideas exist already, but don't appear to us until a time in history when people are more receptive to thinking them. Could one of these theories be the answer or was it just a coincidence?

René Descartes (1596–1650)
Yacob's contemporary in France was considering similar ideas during the European Enlightenment.

Walda Heywat (17th century)
Yacob's pupil also wrote a *hatäta* that built on his teacher's work, but he focused more on practical advice on how to live a good life.

Achille Mbembe (1957–)
A Cameroon philosopher whose ideas include rejecting the Eurocentric view of philosophy that fuelled the forgery debate over Yacob's *Hatäta*.

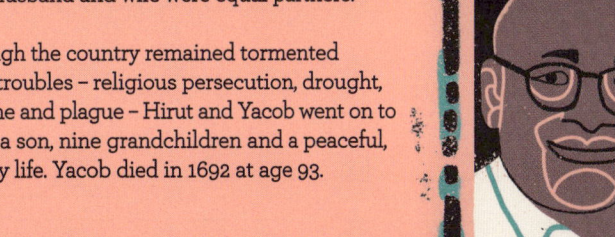

A LONG LIFE

Yacob stayed in Enfraz for the next 60 years. He married a woman named Hirut – a maid at Habtu's household. Habtu offered to give Hirut to Yacob, but Yacob did not want a servant. He wanted an equal, and he believed that husband and wife were equal partners.

Though the country remained tormented with troubles – religious persecution, drought, famine and plague – Hirut and Yacob went on to have a son, nine grandchildren and a peaceful, happy life. Yacob died in 1692 at age 93.

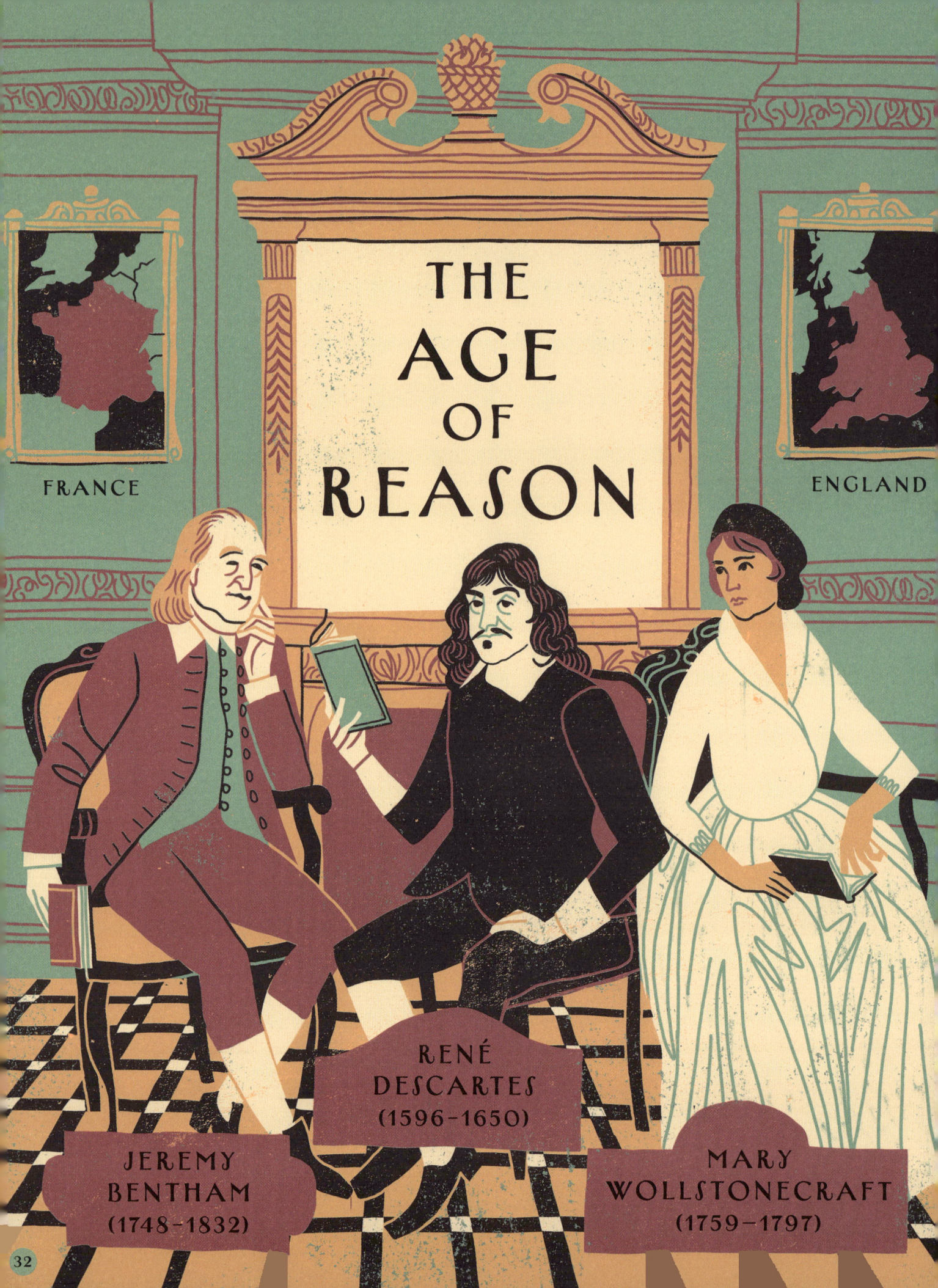

THE MARCH TO MODERNITY

MIDDLE AGES

European society from the 1300s to the 1500s was feudal. That meant that most people were either peasants working the land or craftsmen, all under the control of the nobility and church. Indeed, most ordinary people felt serving the church was their duty, and its spectacular wealth and power during this time was seen in its many grand cathedrals.

THE RENAISSANCE

But changes were afoot. Towards the end of the Middle Ages there was a renaissance, or rebirth, of ancient ideas. This came about from the rediscovery and translation of ancient Greek, Roman and Islamic writings. After the printing press was invented in 1444, these texts were spread (and read!) much more widely.

Absolute religious authority and other ideas laid down by the church began to be questioned. Almost all areas of European society saw change, from art, architecture and music to banking, politics, medicine and religion.

THE SCIENTIFIC REVOLUTION

From the 1600s, scientific methods such as observation and measurement were used to explain the natural world. This was when Galileo first sighted the moons of Jupiter through his telescope and Isaac Newton described ground-breaking laws of physics. In short, this was a time of enormous and exciting scientific discoveries. But sharing these discoveries was still dangerous: the church saw them as a threat to its authority.

AGE OF EXPLORATION

And it wasn't just European societies that changed. From the 1400s, with improved skills in navigation, European traders and seafarers visited six of the world's seven continents, only missing Antarctica.

Europe's trade and wealth was boosted by new cultural encounters. But its demand for more and more resources, such as sugar, spices and tobacco, led European powers to interfere in the running of other territories. This marked the beginnings of colonialism.

THE AGE OF REASON

Nevertheless, the use of scientific methods spread to other areas of study. By the late 17th century, philosophers and other intellectuals were using them in their search for truth and to answer important questions about how society should be run.

They challenged the assumed God-given rights of kings and queens and laws set down by the Christian religion. Finally, they called the period they were living through the Enlightenment, or the Age of Reason.

AN ENLIGHTENED WORLD

Although this time is often referred to as *the* Enlightenment, there were actually many Enlightenments across Europe and its colonies, especially in the Americas. New ideas were constantly being put forward and advanced by dozens of the most influential philosophers in history. In this chapter, we explore ideas from René Descartes, Jeremy Bentham and Mary Wollstonecraft.

LEARNING WHAT TO KNOW

Is there anything we know for certain?

René Descartes was born in La Haye (now called Descartes!), France, towards the end of the Renaissance in 1596. He attended a very strict Jesuit school where he learned Latin and scholastic philosophy. This philosophy promoted Aristotle's ideas as they seemed to support the Catholic Church.

As a young man, Descartes joined the army and travelled all over Europe experiencing many different cultures. As he discovered different people and ideas, he grew to disagree with much of the philosophy he had learned. Descartes wanted to share his objections but before doing so, he needed to know that his own arguments were based in truth. This led him to ask: is there *anything* we know for certain?

A METHOD OF DOUBT

For knowledge to be reliable it needed, Descartes claimed, to have a reliable foundation, so he devised a method for testing what he knew.

1. Descartes says you must imagine a most evil demon, like this one.

2. This demon wants to trick you into believing things that are untrue.

3. To avoid being tricked, you must question everything you know and everything you see in the world around you. This method of questioning, or doubting, helps you discover what is true and untrue.

This method will lead you to discover the truths which are beyond doubt and are therefore certain. These truths are the foundation for knowledge.

COGITO, ERGO SUM

For Descartes, one thing was beyond doubt: that he himself existed. After all, if he didn't exist, he could not have been thinking about demons or, indeed, anything at all. The act of thinking was evidence for him of his existence: I think, therefore I am. Though Descartes famously said it in Latin.

Cogito, ergo sum.

ARE THE MIND AND BODY SEPARATE?

Having said it was impossible to doubt his own existence, Descartes confusingly went on to say that it was possible to doubt that his body existed. So, if his body didn't exist, then what part of him was the 'I' that did exist?

To Descartes, the 'I' was the thinking part, the mind. This separation of the self into two parts – the mind and the body – shaped all philosophical ideas from Descartes onwards. We call it Cartesian Dualism. Cartesian comes from Descartes' name, and 'dualism' means two opposing parts.

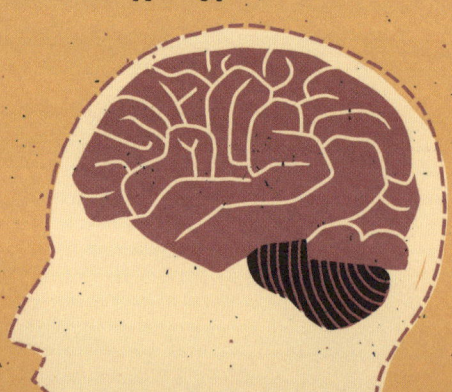

RECOGNISING THE UNSEEABLE

But how can the mind be separate? It doesn't exist on its own; it exists in the body. Let's try a thought experiment:

Picture a whole triangle – a shape with three straight sides.

Now picture a whole chiliagon – a shape with one thousand straight sides.

While you can see a triangle, you *cannot* see the chiliagon and neither can anyone! Although we can't picture it, our minds can *perceive* of one and understand what it is. Descartes concluded that our minds perceive things in two ways:

1. Through senses, based on information from the observable world outside us.

2. Through thought, based on information stored in our brains.

LETTERS TO ELISABETH

Elisabeth Palatine (1618–1680) was the well-educated princess of Bohemia who traded letters with many intellectuals, including Descartes. In 1643, she invited him to tutor her in philosophy. While devising her own theories, Palatine questioned Descartes on his work, helping to sharpen his ideas. He dedicated his book, *Principles of Philosophy*, to Palatine and they corresponded until his death in 1650.

JEREMY BENTHAM'S STORY

Almost a century later across the English Channel, Jeremy Bentham was born in 1748. He grew up in London as the son of a lawyer and from a young age, he studied law with the goal of joining the courts.

But Bentham quickly grew to dislike how both the courts and the country were being run. He complained that the legal system was unfair and that the government interfered too much in people's lives instead of helping them become responsible citizens.

This dislike got Bentham thinking: how could society change for the better? He decided that the way to do this was to increase pleasure and minimise pain, which sounds great, doesn't it? Bentham thought long and hard about how this principle could work throughout all of society and he came up with an idea. He called it utilitarianism.

UTILITARIANISM

Bentham said that actions that result in pleasure or happiness, or help to prevent pain or unhappiness, are morally good. How much goodness an action brings about is its utility.

Utility would allow all human actions to be judged on the amount of happiness they bring about, versus the amount of pain they cause to everyone involved, now and in the future. Bentham argued that this utilitarian system would guarantee the greatest happiness for the greatest number of people.

UTILITY IN ACTION

Imagine you're asked to litter pick in the park instead of playing with your friends. If you pick litter, the park will be clean, making it safer for people and wildlife for days to come. But, in the moment, you lose out on having fun with your friends.

Utilitarianism says that you should pick up the litter because it will bring the greatest good for the greatest number of people. Would you do it? Should you?

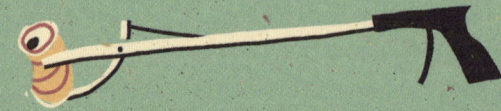

THE PANOPTICON

Bentham thought to apply his utilitarian theory to crime and punishment in order to make it work better. Since all punishment causes pain, which to Bentham was morally bad, he said it should only be used to prevent even greater suffering.

He and his brother Samuel, an engineer, spent 20 years designing a model prison building called the Panopticon. Here's how it works:

A single watchman could see all the prisoners from a tower in the middle, but no prisoner could see the watchman. Each prisoner could assume that they were being watched at any time, so they would then behave all the time as if they were being watched.

In this prison, no officer would cause harm to a prisoner, and prisoners would police themselves into being good both inside and outside of prison.

BECOMING AN 'AUTO-ICON'

Bentham's ideas led to the founding of England's first secular university, University College London (UCL). His body even remains there to this day...

In his essay 'Farther Uses of the Dead to the Living', Bentham suggested that after death, a person's body should be donated to medical science to help the greater good. Remains should be turned into an 'auto-icon' stuffed with straw, preserved and dressed for display.

After his death in 1832, his utilitarian wish was granted. His body was dissected and his auto-icon – topped with a wax head – was created. It is kept at UCL in a glass cabinet and trundled out for special occasions!

THE MINDS OF WOMEN

Much of the philosophy that came during the Enlightenment about the mind and body, basic rights, laws, happiness and so on was focused on men. Clearly, at this time, it was much harder for women – even those born into wealth or privilege – to take part in society's intellectual conversations. Their inputs were often ignored on the supposed grounds that women's minds were inferior to those of men.

THE WORLD OF MARY WOLLSTONECRAFT

Mary Wollstonecraft was born in London, England, in 1759, not too far from Bentham. However, unlike Bentham, Wollstonecraft was not born into wealth – in fact, her father had squandered their family fortune. While she didn't attend school, the young Wollstonecraft learned to read in Dutch, French and German, and was introduced to some ancient Greek writings as well as the Bible. Later, after working as a teacher and governess, she was paid to translate important texts, including some works of philosophy.

WOMEN AND RATIONAL THOUGHT

Often in her line of work, Wollstonecraft encountered negative attitudes towards women, so she challenged them. Throughout her career she wrote several books, the most famous being *A Vindication of the Rights of Woman*, published in 1792. In this book, Wollstonecraft set out a clear, reasoned argument to show that women are every bit as rational as men. This was, after all, the Age of Reason!

THE BLANK SLATE

Another famous Enlightenment philosopher, John Locke (1632–1704), influenced Wollstonecraft's ideas. Locke believed people are born without any knowledge at all – in his words, we are *tabula rasas* or blank slates. All our knowledge comes from our experiences – from the world to which we are exposed in our upbringing and education.

But when Locke said 'people', he was only referring to men. Wollstonecraft argued that Locke's blank slate idea was true of women too, and that it also applied to intellectual ability. How could women possibly do as well as men if they were treated as inferior from birth? It was girls' education that was inferior, not girls themselves.

PROGRESS FOR WOMEN AND WOMEN FOR PROGRESS

Crucially, part of Wollstonecraft's argument was aimed at women. She urged them not to fall into society's trap which forced them into inferiority. This trap made women believe they were less clever and capable than men.

But more than this, Enlightenment society needed to remove the trap. Wollstonecraft argued that freedom of women was vital for progress, and that failing to teach girls to the same level as boys would threaten this progress – and even stop it altogether.

> *My own sex, I hope, will excuse me, if I treat them like rational creatures, instead of... viewing them as if they were in a state of perpetual childhood, unable to stand alone.*

A SHORT LIFE BUT A LONG-LASTING LEGACY

Wollstonecraft died aged 38, 11 days after giving birth to her second child (who would grow up to become Mary Shelley, the author of *Frankenstein*). Considered as one of the earliest feminist writers, her powerful argument for the equality of women and men, particularly when it came to matters of the mind, was truly enlightening.

Gilbert Ryle (1900–1976)
A British thinker who challenged Cartesian Dualism, calling the separation of the mind from the body a 'ghost in the machine'.

John Stewart Mill (1806–1873)
Another famous Enlightenment philosopher who valued happiness and utilitarianism.

Emilie du Châtelet (1706–1749)
This French natural philosopher critiqued both Descartes and Locke, and had her own ideas about how we know things.

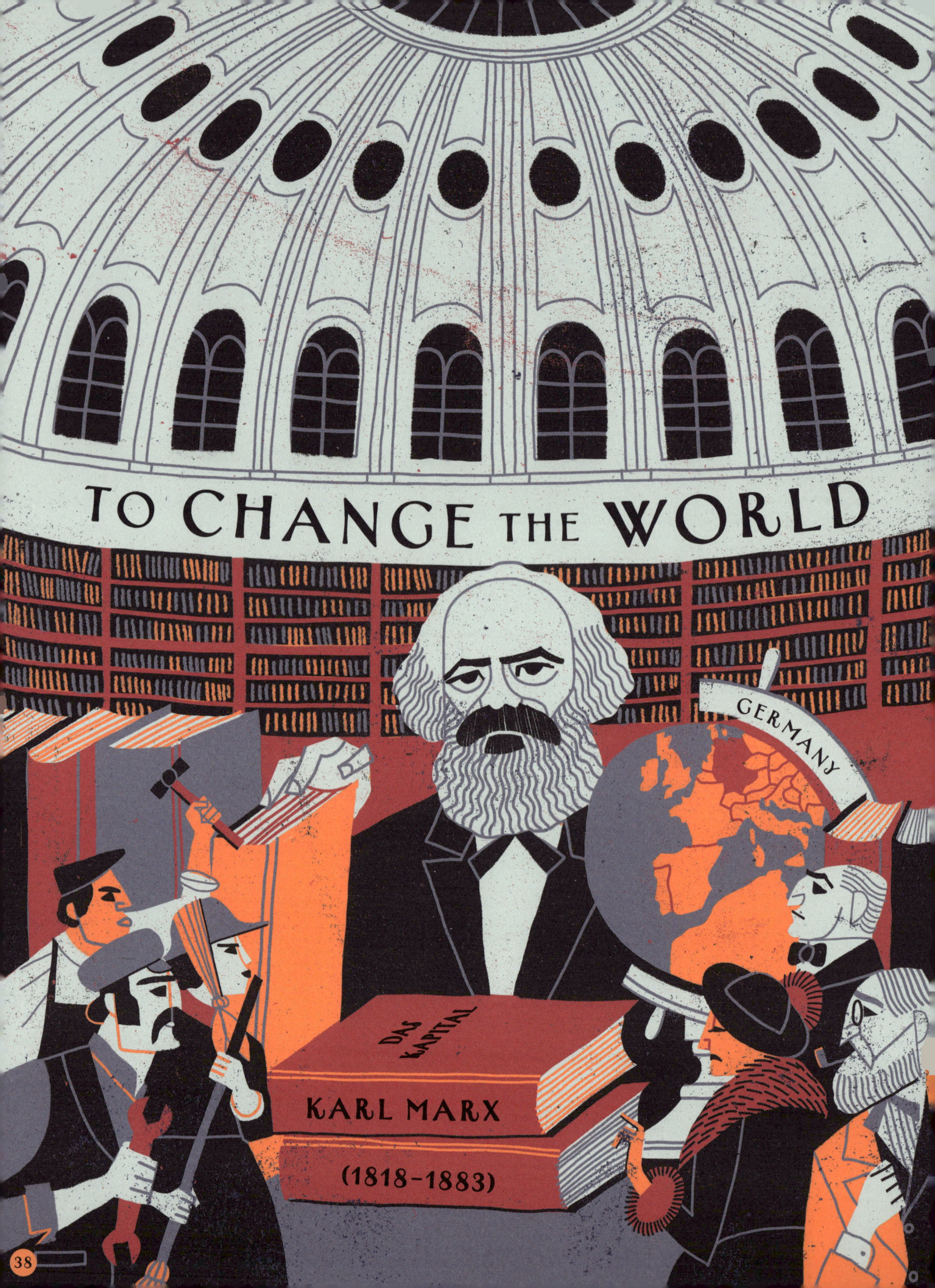

AN EXPLOSIVE TIME

Wars, radical new inventions, thousands of people on the move and centuries-old ways of life being overturned – Europe was going through a time of unprecedented upheaval and change.

1789–1799
The French Revolution challenged the rule of the rich and a new republic arose.

1801–1815
The Napoleonic Wars ravaged many European countries.

1804
The world population soared to 1 billion.

1845–1849
The Irish Potato Famine left around 1 million people dead, and 1 million more emigrated, mostly to North America.

1834
Slavery was finally banned throughout the British Empire.

1853–1856
The Crimean War fatally weakend the Russian Empire.

1859
Charles Darwin's theory of evolution challenged the understanding of humanity's place in the world.

1861–1865
The American Civil War marked the end of slavery and the birth of a new USA.

1867
Alfred Nobel invented dynamite, revolutionising mining, industry and warfare all over the world.

THE INDUSTRIAL REVOLUTION

During this momentous time, another kind of revolution was happening. Beginning in Britain, the Industrial Revolution was an age of machines fuelled by the invention of steam power. Thousands of people moved to the cities to work, bound to factories spewing black smoke day and night. Men, women and children worked long hours underground, mining coal to feed the new trains, mills and factories. For some, technological progress heralded an exciting new age. For others, life steadily worsened.

KARL MARX'S STORY

Karl Marx was born in 1818 in Trier, present-day Germany. After university, he travelled around Europe working as a journalist. Wherever he went, Marx was drawn to groups of people who saw unfairness in the world and had ideas to change it. However, he was always forced to move on when the authorities became suspicious of these groups' plans.

In 1843, he married activist Jenny von Westphalen and they had seven children, though four died in childhood. From 1849 they lived in London, which was a refuge for people who disagreed with those in power. The family was poor, often depending on Marx's friend Friedrich Engels to put food on the table.

Every day, Marx trudged through London to the British Library where he worked on his most famous book, *Das Kapital*. This was a huge, rambling study of the time he lived in and why he believed it needed to change. Marx never managed to finish the book because, like now, the world he was trying to describe kept changing.

WORK AND HOW IT CHANGED

Marx was constantly scribbling his ideas down, but his handwriting was terrible. Fortunately, Jenny and Engels were able to decipher his scrawl and make readable copies of his work. Jointly with Engels, he wrote a short pamphlet called The Communist Manifesto, published in 1848. The pamphlet described the system that Marx saw at work in the world. This system was capitalism. Marx didn't think this system was fair to everyone, so he argued for a new one: communism.

proletariat – *the working class*

bourgeoisie – *the ruling class*

HOW CAPITALISM WORKS

Marx explained capitalism as a system where a class of people called the bourgeoisie rule society. This is because they own objects and materials called the means of production. Another much larger class called the proletariat are the workers. They work for the bourgeoisie by making goods which are sold for profit. The bourgeoisie receive most of the profit and the workers get a small amount in the form of wages.

means of production – *things like factory buildings, machines, raw materials – what you need to make things to sell*

profit – *the money made from selling an item for more than it cost to make*

WORK AND HOW IT CHANGED

To Marx, capitalism was a problem for the working class for two key reasons. Firstly, their work was unsatisfying and disconnected workers from what made them human. Secondly, they were being exploited to make profit for the ruling class.

In the past, people made objects from scratch to either sell or use. Marx said this was fulfilling because people used their skills and creativity – parts of themselves – in their work. But in capitalist factories, workers only made one piece of an object over and over, as if they were machines. The work was boring and because workers had no say in the final product, they became detached from their work and their humanity.

Also, long hours operating hazardous machinery was very dangerous. If workers' attention wandered, horrible injuries and even death could result – and it often did. The bourgeoisie did very little to assure workers' safety in their factories.

Finally, at the end of the process, the workers did not own what they had made. Instead, they were forced to use their meagre wages to buy objects and often found they couldn't afford them at all. While the bourgeoisie grew richer under this system, the proletariat became poorer and owned less.

WHAT'S PHILOSOPHY FOR?

Marx said it was not the philosopher's job just to explain the world to us – instead philosophers should change the world for the better. But can ideas only be good if they create practical change?

HOW COMMUNISM WORKS

The idea of communism has been around for centuries. Marx's version calls for ending the struggle between bourgeoisie and proletariat by making a classless society. To do this, the means of production needed to be owned by everyone. Marx wanted a society where people could develop freely, not one where making profit was the main goal. By sharing all the resources, people would be able to try different things instead of doing the same job over and over. The chance to try different things, Marx believed, was part of being human.

MARXISM IN PRACTICE

Marxism (the name for Marx's ideas), communism and socialism are all similar ideas about how people should work and live. Some countries have declared themselves to be Marxist, communist or socialist and said they follow Marx's ideals, but in reality their resources were not owned by everyone. Instead, dictators had absolute control over the people and resources, like Joseph Stalin (1878–1953) in the USSR or Mao Zedong (1893–1976) in China. What might Marx have said about these dictators' versions of communism?

THE SAME EVERYWHERE

Marx saw how capitalism was starting to make everywhere feel the same, causing countries to lose their individual characters. Now, over 170 years later, the same coffee and clothing shops can be found in many cities around the world. Can you think of some? Do you know any cafes or shops that are unique? For many countries, the struggle to retain their individual identity under capitalism is ongoing.

MARX'S LEGACY

Marx didn't think that the world he saw – one shaped by capitalism – was permanent. He strongly believed that things could change. Marx left no detailed plan for a communist future because he thought the world would evolve that way naturally. Since Marx's death in 1883, many countries have experimented with putting his ideas into practice with mixed success. But, supported by Marx's vision, the fight for workers' rights, fairness and equality continues.

Adam Smith (1723–1790)
An economist who argued governments should not interfere in a country's economy.

Eleanor Marx (1855–1898)
Marx's youngest daughter built on her father's ideas. She campaigned for an eight-hour workday, especially for children.

Angela Davis (1944–)
A Black American philosopher and activist, passionate about Marxist ideas.

INDIA

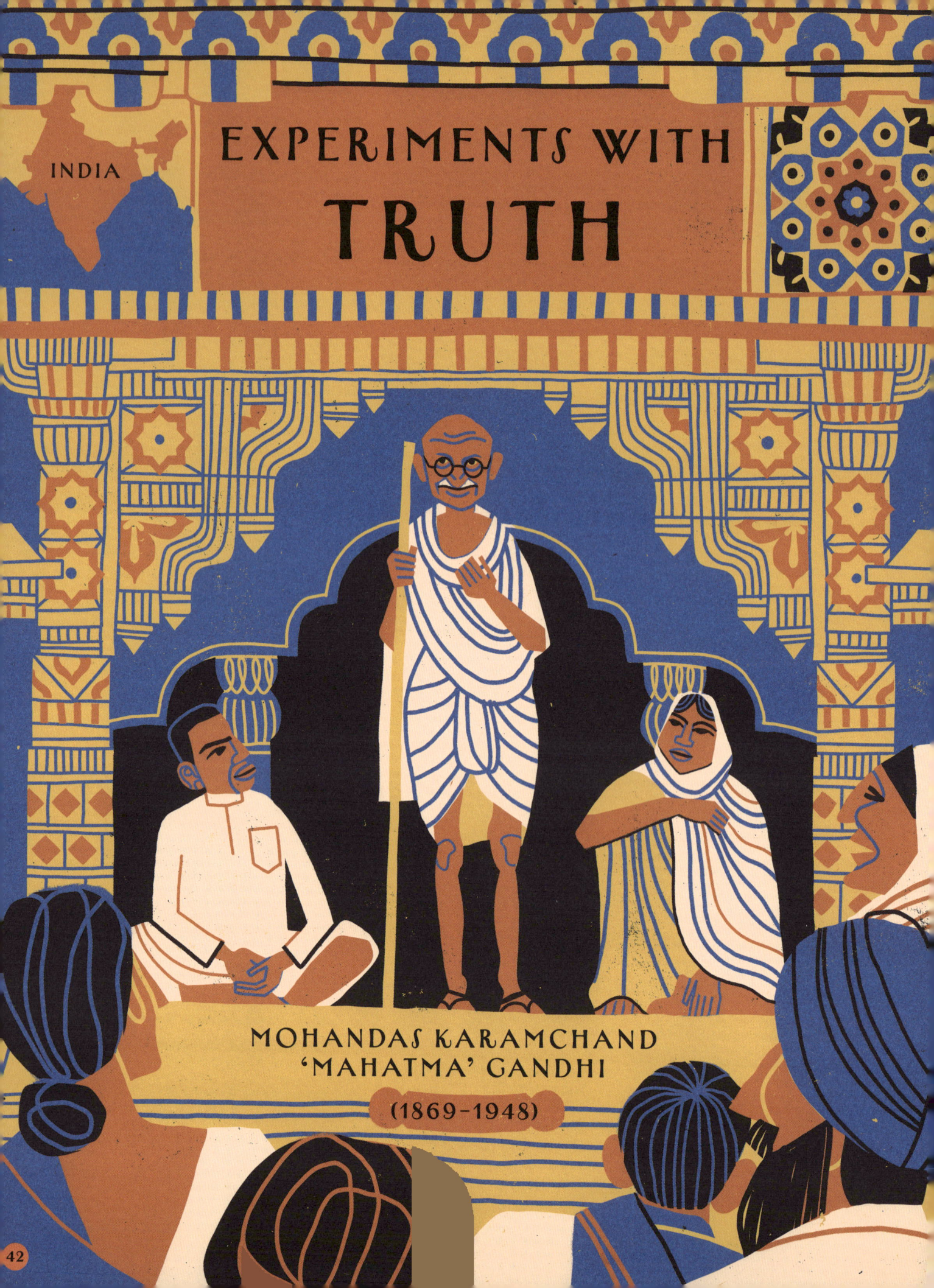

EXPERIMENTS WITH TRUTH

MOHANDAS KARAMCHAND 'MAHATMA' GANDHI

(1869–1948)

THE BRITISH IN INDIA

The British Raj or rule of India officially lasted from 1858 to 1947, but the economic and political invasion of the land had started long before. From the early 17th century, the British East India Company had used bribes, treaties, threats and their private army to gain access to the Indian subcontinent's spices, cotton cloth, tea and opium.

DIVIDE AND CONQUER

Part of what made this takeover possible was the sheer size of India. It was home to many clashing kingdoms, religious groups and cultures. The British made use of a tactic called divide and conquer, fanning the flames of disagreement between the many groups to turn them against each other instead of the British. Over time, it became understood to many British people that Britain owned India, and that the British were the superior masters ruling over the Indian servants.

GANDHI'S STORY

Gandhi was born in 1869 in Porbandar, India, to a Hindu family. At school he was an average student who had awful handwriting and was painfully shy.

He married Kasturba when they were 13. They had five children, though sadly their first baby died.

Gandhi wanted to be a doctor, but his father disapproved so he travelled to London to study to become a lawyer.

He tried to fit in by dressing and acting like an English gentleman, but it was hard to keep up. Having promised his mother not to eat meat, he struggled to find vegetarian restaurants.

In 1891, Gandhi returned to India, then in 1893 he moved to South Africa to practise law. There he was the victim of discrimination.

For 21 years, he fought to improve conditions for Indians in South Africa, organising large civil disobedience campaigns and using his skills as a lawyer to fight racist government bills.

When Gandhi returned to settle in India, he became convinced that for India and its citizens to thrive, it must become an independent country. This was called *Swaraj* (swah-rahj) or 'Home Rule'.

He looked for ways to become self-sufficient. Gandhi taught Indians hand spinning, and encouraged them to boycott imported British cloth.

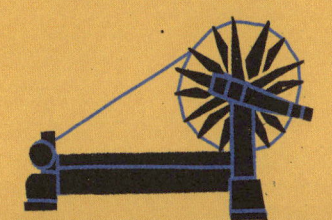

In 1922, because of the boycott, Gandhi was sentenced to prison for six years but was released after two because of his health. In his lifetime, Gandhi was arrested 11 times, spending nearly 7 years in jail.

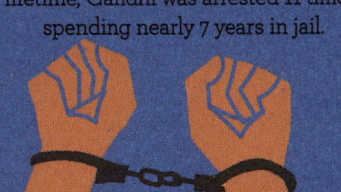

Gandhi's experiences and the people and ideas he came across led him to a philosophy that would win India its freedom.

THREE WORDS TO LIVE BY

Throughout his life, Gandhi felt he made many mistakes, but he always did his best to learn from them. In his autobiography, *The Story of My Experiments with Truth*, Gandhi describes the different ideas he tested in his search for how to live a good and kind life. These experiments led him to a commitment to three principles, which he tried to live by in both his private and public life.

AHIMSA

Ahimsa (ah-him-sa) means 'non-injury'. Gandhi thought it was important to live a non-violent life. This didn't just mean non-violence to other humans, but to all life, which is why he chose not to eat meat.

TAPASYA

Tapasya (tah-pah-see-yah) means 'self-suffering'. Gandhi's philosophy required him and his followers to be willing to accept losing their homes, being sent to prison, being beaten or even dying if they had to, in order to achieve justice.

SATYAGRAHA

Satyagraha (satyee-ah-gra-ha) means 'holding firm to truth' or, as Gandhi sometimes said, 'truth-force'. Truth was at the heart of Gandhi's philosophy and in everything he did.

ASKING THE RIGHT QUESTIONS

Gandhi's followers questioned how these principles would lead to *Swaraj*.

Is this how we'll beat our enemy?

Is this how we're going to win?

Will this drive the British out?

For Gandhi, these were the wrong questions to ask. They weren't trying to win or beat their enemy. They were trying to understand the truth of an evil situation and in sharing that understanding with their opponents, encourage them to rethink their actions and have a change of heart.

But how do we come to understand truth?

Through his own experience, Gandhi believed that the way to understand the truth was through self-purification, which meant eliminating negative feelings and actions in your life and heart.

Gandhi taught his followers to:

1. Live simply and be self-sufficient.
2. Eat sparingly, causing no harm to animals.
3. Not be obsessed with possessions.
4. Harbour no ill thoughts towards others.

Living in this way gave Gandhi and his followers the inner strength to take the ideals of *ahimsa*, *tapasya* and *satyagraha* – non-violence, self-suffering and truth-force – and turn them into action.

MAHATMA AND BAPU

Gandhi is often known as Mahatma Gandhi. *Mahatma* means 'great soul' in Sanskrit. The name made him feel uncomfortable, Gandhi said, because he didn't think he deserved it. He was happier with the title *Bapu* or 'beloved father', because he believed a father could have flaws.

PEOPLE NEED SALT TO LIVE

The 1882 Salt Act banned Indians from collecting or selling salt. Instead, they were forced to buy it from the British, who taxed this essential item heavily. This was particularly hard on the poor. Gandhi decided in 1930 that salt could be a powerful focus for a non-violent protest.

THE MARCH TO THE SEA

Satyagraha requires honesty even to your enemy, so Gandhi wrote to the authorities to tell them about the planned Salt March.

On 12 March 1930, Gandhi left his home with a small group of followers, beginning the long trek to the sea to collect illegal salt from the salt flats. In 24 days, they walked 385 kilometres.

At each night's resting place, Gandhi gave speeches about the way forward for India. Many more Indians joined the march, which grew to be 50,000 strong.

THE JOURNEY

Reporters and film crews from around the world flocked to cover the march and influenced opinions about Britain's continued rule of India.

When he arrived at the sea, Gandhi bent down and broke the law by picking up a piece of mud-encrusted salt, watched by thousands of his followers. It was a powerful moment.

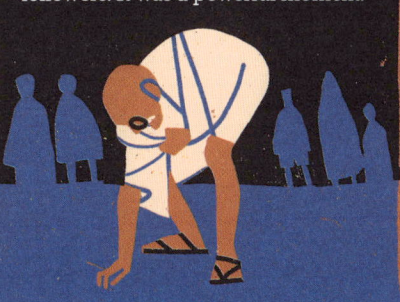

Across India, people began to make their own salt, defying the British law.

During the following year, around 60,000 Indians were arrested, including Gandhi.

SALT RIGHTS ARE GRANTED BY BRITAIN
Gandhi Wins Nationalists Freedom From Monopoly After Long Parley

WHAT HAPPENED AFTER THE SALT MARCH?

The Salt March succeeded in changing the law, but it took 17 more years and many campaigns and hardships before India gained its independence. In 1947, to Gandhi's sorrow, his country was divided into the separate nations of India and Pakistan. Not long after, Gandhi was shot dead by a Hindu extremist who deeply distrusted Gandhi's religious tolerance. Around a million people lined the road as Gandhi's body was taken to be cremated.

GANDHI'S LEGACY

Gandhi's philosophy offered a way of responding to injustice in the world. Gandhi knew it wouldn't be simple and saw *satyagraha* as an ongoing process in each of us, out of which non-violent action can arise. His ideas remain to this day a philosophical and political challenge to individuals and leaders alike.

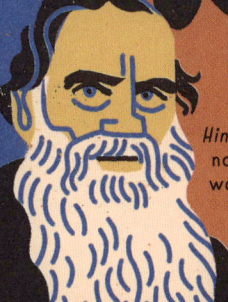

Leo Tolstoy (1828–1910)
In *A Letter to a Hindu*, he argued that non-violent protest was the way to free India from the British. This greatly influenced Gandhi, and he and Tolstoy wrote back and forth.

Albert Einstein (1879–1955)
The famous scientist greatly admired Gandhi's commitment to non-violence. Einstein even had a picture of Gandhi on his study wall.

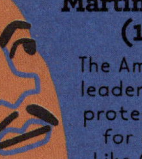

Martin Luther King Jr (1929–1968)
The American civil rights leader used non-violent protest in the struggle for racial equality. Like Gandhi, King was assassinated.

(1870–1945)

THE EXISTENCE OF NOTHING

JAPAN

西田 幾多郎

NISHIDA KITARŌ

THE MEIJI AND THE MAKING OF MODERN JAPAN

Nishida Kitarō was born in 1870 in Unoke, a small, quiet village on the Sea of Japan. The country had recently emerged from the strict military dictatorship of the Tokugawa period (1603–1867) and change was afoot. Under the Tokugawa, Japanese society had been organised into a rigid class system. It had also isolated itself from the rest of the world and, in particular, Christian and European influences.

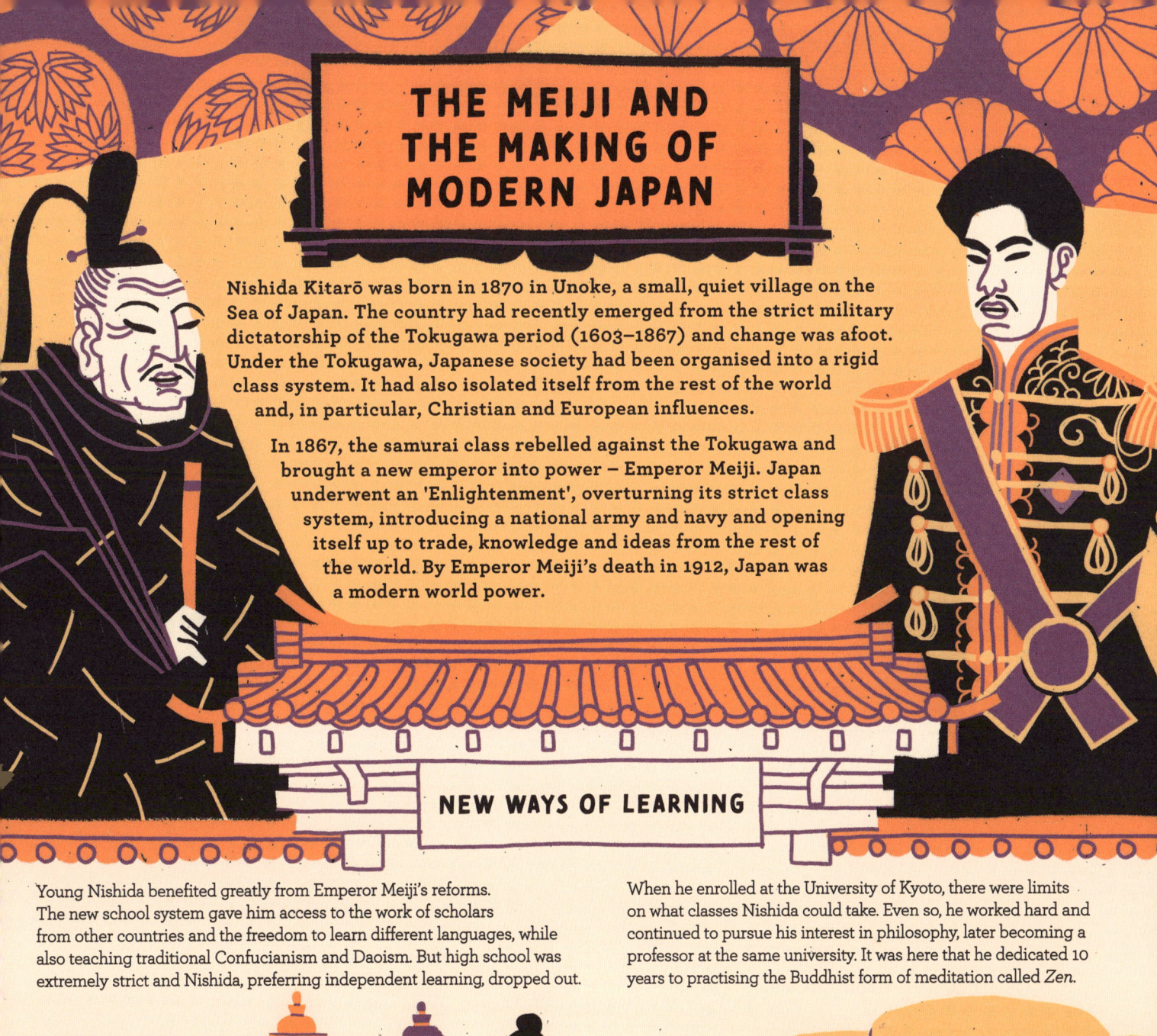

In 1867, the samurai class rebelled against the Tokugawa and brought a new emperor into power – Emperor Meiji. Japan underwent an 'Enlightenment', overturning its strict class system, introducing a national army and navy and opening itself up to trade, knowledge and ideas from the rest of the world. By Emperor Meiji's death in 1912, Japan was a modern world power.

NEW WAYS OF LEARNING

Young Nishida benefited greatly from Emperor Meiji's reforms. The new school system gave him access to the work of scholars from other countries and the freedom to learn different languages, while also teaching traditional Confucianism and Daoism. But high school was extremely strict and Nishida, preferring independent learning, dropped out.

When he enrolled at the University of Kyoto, there were limits on what classes Nishida could take. Even so, he worked hard and continued to pursue his interest in philosophy, later becoming a professor at the same university. It was here that he dedicated 10 years to practising the Buddhist form of meditation called *Zen*.

BUDDHA AND THE MEANING OF LIFE

Buddhism is a religion that follows the teachings of Siddhārtha Gautama, known as Gautama Buddha. He lived in Nepal from around 563 to 483 BCE.

The son of a king, Gautama had all the earthly possessions he could desire, but he was not satisfied. Although he had everything, he did not know the meaning of life.

One stormy night, Gautama left his palace and the people he loved in search of the answer. He joined a group of people called ascetics who believed that denying themselves belongings and pleasures would bring a higher understanding. But after years of denying himself comforts, he still didn't know the meaning of life, so he continued his journey.

One day, Gautama stopped to rest and meditate under a fig tree. He meditated for 49 days, reaching a state of mental and spiritual purity called enlightenment. He became the 'Buddha' – the enlightened one – and began to share his understanding with others.

BUDDHISM, TRUTH AND ZEN

Followers of Buddha's teachings are known as Buddhists. As part of their learning journey, Buddhists practise *Zen*. Although *Zen* is a Japanese translation of *Chán*, the Chinese word for meditation, it means more than that. *Zen* involves contemplating curious riddles or challenges called *koan*, designed to free the mind from logic and ego.

Here's an example of *koan*: How can you hold the plough with empty hands? Take hold of the plough with both your hands.

Zen

Koan

MORE QUESTIONS THAN ANSWERS

Compelled by Buddha's story, Nishida wanted to practise *Zen* to reach enlightenment. During his meditations, he reached a state in which his body and mind felt at one with the world around him – as if he was everything, but also nothing. But rather than giving Nishida the answers to existence, practising *Zen* led him to ask more questions about how we experience reality.

What is our 'self' in the world? What is the nature of reality? Does reality exist without people to experience it?

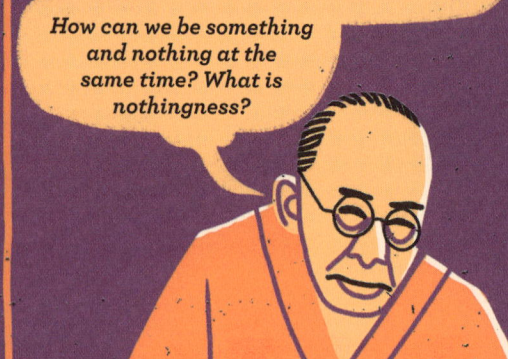

How can we be something and nothing at the same time? What is nothingness?

REFLECTING ON 'SELF' IN THE WORLD

Look into a mirror. What do you see? You probably see yourself and the things in the room that you are in at this moment. But the image is not your real self: it is a reflection.

Nishida thought that people experienced all of existence as a sort-of reflection. Each person can only see as far as their consciousness and unique position will allow, but they are nevertheless looking at the same, objective reality as everyone else. He called this objective reality the 'pure experience', and it exists whether or not people gaze upon it.

By meditating, Nishida said we can feel at one with the world around us and we can lose our sense of self. This is true awakening to reality in its pure, rather than reflected, state.

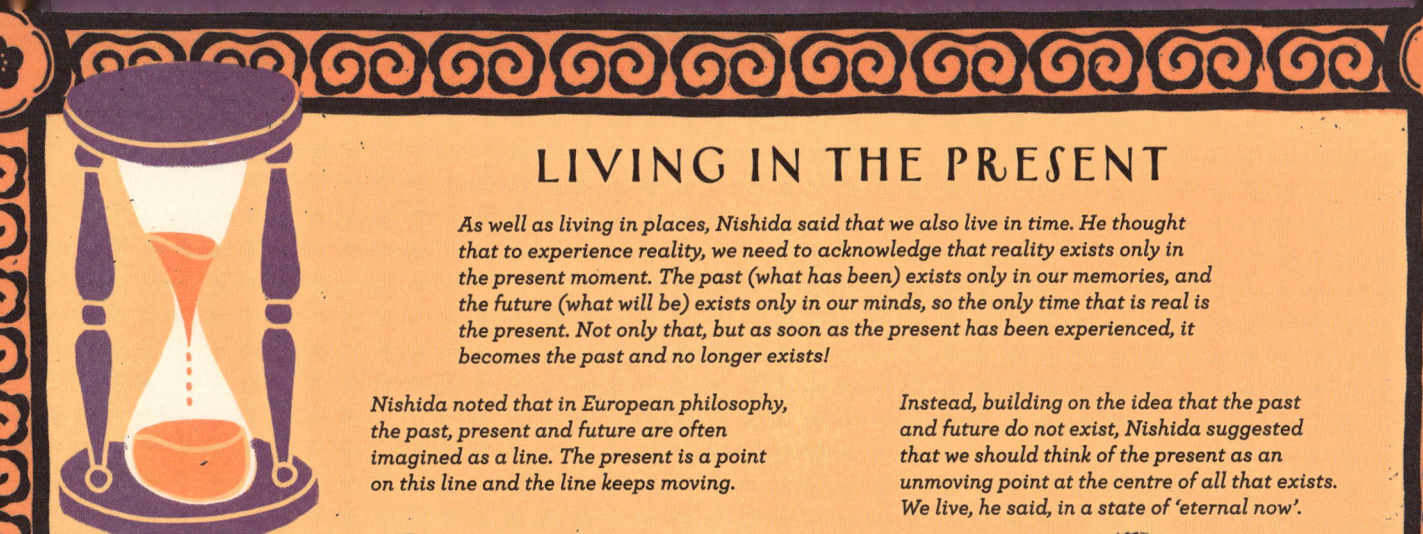

LIVING IN THE PRESENT

As well as living in places, Nishida said that we also live in time. He thought that to experience reality, we need to acknowledge that reality exists only in the present moment. The past (what has been) exists only in our memories, and the future (what will be) exists only in our minds, so the only time that is real is the present. Not only that, but as soon as the present has been experienced, it becomes the past and no longer exists!

Nishida noted that in European philosophy, the past, present and future are often imagined as a line. The present is a point on this line and the line keeps moving.

Instead, building on the idea that the past and future do not exist, Nishida suggested that we should think of the present as an unmoving point at the centre of all that exists. We live, he said, in a state of 'eternal now'.

Past Present Future   Eternal now

HOW CAN NOTHING EXIST?

The idea that you can lose your sense of self in the present through meditation fascinated Nishida. For him, it meant that the starting place for thought was the non-self, rather than the thinking self of modern Western philosophy (much like Descartes suggested). But how can the non-self exist? Does that mean our thoughts come from nothing? Well, according to Nishida, they do!

Nishida's idea of nothing was the opposite of European existentialism, a philosophy which said 'nothing' is the nonexistence of all objects, time, space, thought – the nonexistence of all things. Instead, influenced by Buddhist teachings, Nishida thought of nothingness – or *Mu* – as the coming together of all those things. All existence, he said, is surrounded by and created from an unknowable reality, an absolute nothingness. So while some European philosophers, such as Jean-Paul Sartre, feared 'nothing', Nishida thought that there was nothing to fear!

NISHIDA'S LEGACY

Nishida brought together *Zen* and European philosophies, combining cultures to create a new approach to ideas about reality and nothingness. His department became known as the Kyoto School, and he retired in 1930. But retirement did not stop him being a philosopher. Most of his work was made between 1930 and 1945 when he died. Long after, Nishida's ideas stir philosophical debate worldwide and his birthplace hosts the largest building in the world dedicated to a single philosopher, which is definitely *not* nothing!

無 *Mu*

D.T. Suzuki (1870–1966)
A Japanese-American philosopher and Buddhist monk who popularised *Zen*.

Friedrich Nietzsche (1844–1900)
This German philosopher had a different approach to 'nothingness' called nihilism.

Martin Heidegger (1889–1976)
A German philosopher with huge influence inside and outside philosophy who wrote about the relationship between time and existence.

WE ARE THE SYMBOL MAKERS

SUSANNE LANGER
(1895–1985)

SUSANNE LANGER'S STORY

Susanne Knauth was born in the cultural melting pot that was New York City in 1895, as the second of five children. Her parents were well-off German immigrants and their house was full of books, music and lively discussions. As a child, Susanne was accidentally poisoned, so much of her early education happened at home.

Indoors, her creativity flourished as she wrote stories and plays for her siblings and discovered her love for the cello – an instrument she would enjoy playing her whole life. Although Susanne wished to study, her father didn't think his daughters should go to university. But after his death in 1915, she enrolled in Radcliffe College, and in 1921 she married William Langer and had two sons.

A TRAILBLAZER

At a time when philosophers and professors were almost all men, Langer was one of the first American women to have a career in philosophy. She taught at respected universities and colleges across the country, and in her classes, she refused to just repeat what other thinkers had said.

Some theories of the past, Langer thought, were tired and worn out. She argued that we needed not just new answers to the world's biggest questions, but new questions to ask as well. In her area of study, called aesthetics, she built on the ideas of earlier thinkers, then pushed them further with her own theories about the way our minds work and the place of creativity in our lives.

WHAT IS AESTHETICS?

For as long as people have existed, we have doodled drawings, hummed tunes and moved to a beat. Aesthetics is a type of philosophy that asks questions about why that is, what it means and why we even value art at all.

What makes something beautiful?

Does art say things that are true?

Does everybody think the same things are beautiful?

Why does this object make me feel like this?

If I wasn't looking at it, would this art still be beautiful?

Can looking at something beautiful help make me good?

This is really expensive – does that mean it's beautiful?

WHAT IS ART?

When Langer said 'art', she wasn't just talking about paintings. She also meant music, dance, poetry, sculpture – really any creative activity that translates what's inside of us so that it exists outside of us. Things that we feel, like happiness, can become things we and others can see or hear, like a happy dance or song.

HAVE YOU EVER LISTENED TO A PIECE OF MUSIC, LOOKED AT A PICTURE, READ A POEM OR DANCED WHEN NO ONE WAS LOOKING AND FELT THINGS YOU COULDN'T FIND THE WORDS FOR?

WE ARE SYMBOL MAKING CREATURES

Even if you can't describe something using words, that doesn't mean it can't exist. Langer said this is why we use symbols – they help us understand and express feelings and ideas that ordinary language can't. In fact, she believed that making and using symbols is an essential part of what makes us human. Even though many animals use languages of their own to express themselves in the outer world, humans, Langer said, are the only beings to find meanings for our inner world using symbols.

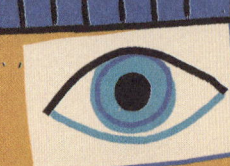

OBJECTIVE AND SUBJECTIVE

Something objective exists in the world in a way that we can see, hear, touch, smell or taste, and describe with words – like this book or a leaf or a birthday cake.

Something subjective, on the other hand, exists inside our minds. It is something we feel but can't describe, like anger or fear. Yet these feelings are recognisable to others even though they are unique to each of us and grow out of our individual experiences.

As humans, we exist in both the outer and the inner world, and we need to try to understand them both to live fully. Science gives us the tools to explore the outer world, but the way we share and understand the inner world is through art.

WHAT IS A SYMBOL?

A symbol is a way of explaining something by using something else. Take this metaphor for example: 'The road was a ribbon of moonlight.' In everyday language you could say 'the road was lit by the moon', but you would lose the shivery, glimmery feelings and imagery of the symbolic language.

The everyday language is factual – it describes what we see happening in the outside world. But the symbol, the metaphor, explains the feelings the writer is trying to pass on from their inside world. Through the symbol, we also recognise those feelings in our inside world – it makes us feel something too.

Langer would say the information that the everyday language gives us is objective, and the feeling the metaphor gives us is subjective. These are the words Langer used to describe different aspects of reality.

CAN ART MAKE US GOOD?

Though Langer wasn't writing about how to live a good life, she did think that to be truly human we need to engage with our feelings. She wondered if it's possible to live a good life if you aren't in touch with all of yourself.

In many schools around the world, art, music and drama are subjects under threat of being cancelled because some people don't believe they offer us anything, unlike science or maths, which give us new technological advances. But Langer believed we needed both science and art to understand life.

THE STUDIO AND THE GALLERY

Langer said that understanding philosophy of art should start in the studio, not in the art gallery. What she meant was that by doing something creative, like drawing a picture of a solitary tree when you're feeling lonely or writing a poem about how much you love your cat, we can truly experience those feelings through using symbols, rather than just keeping them inside of us. Also, by creating art, we are educating our feelings. Then, when we go somewhere like an art gallery, we can use what we have learned to recognise and make sense of what we see there.

FOSSIL LEAF

Philosophers aren't the only ones who appreciate Langer's ideas. In 1987, biologists Jack Wolfe and Wes Wehr named a fossil leaf *Langeria magnifica* after Susanne Langer, in admiration of the way her work saw the place of both art and science.

What would you choose to have named after you?

WORKING TO THE LAST

Even though she was losing her sight, Langer went on writing almost to the end of her life. Her last work was a huge study of the mind and the ways our feelings relate to our thoughts, called *Mind: An Essay on Human Feeling*. Susanne Langer died in 1985 at the age of 89, and even now, every time we doodle, hum or move to a beat, we are taking part in her vision of what it is to be human.

Marshall McLuhan (1911–1980)
A Canadian thinker who wrote about how modern media relates to being human. He described how the way a thought is presented can have a bigger effect on us than the thought itself.

Hannah Arendt (1906–1975)
A German-born American philosopher who looked at what happens when we think about unanswerable questions and how they lead to works of art.

Grayson Perry (1960–)
A popular British artist who believes everyone needs art to help them make sense of the world.

THE TROLLEY PROBLEM

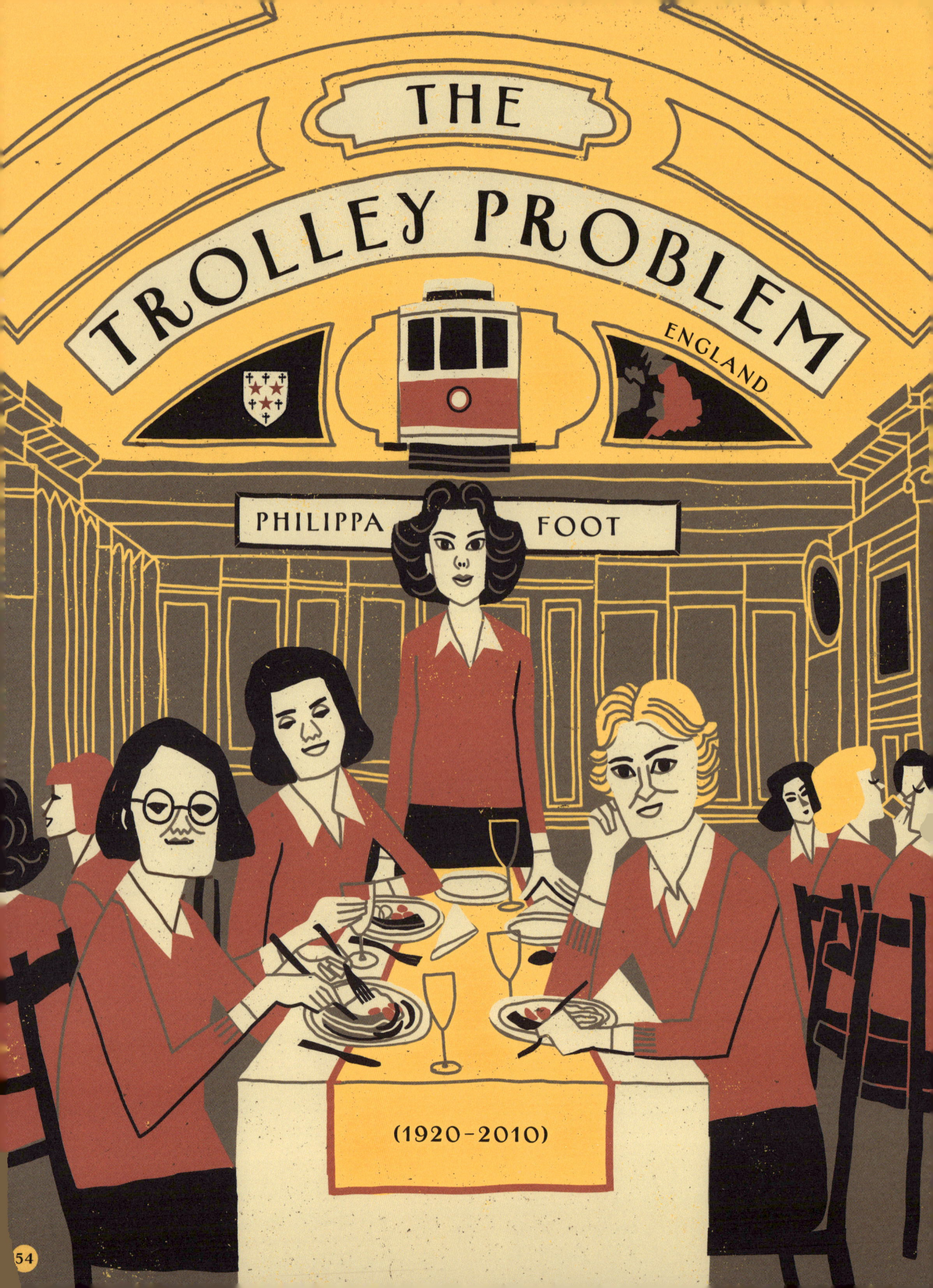

ENGLAND

PHILIPPA FOOT

(1920–2010)

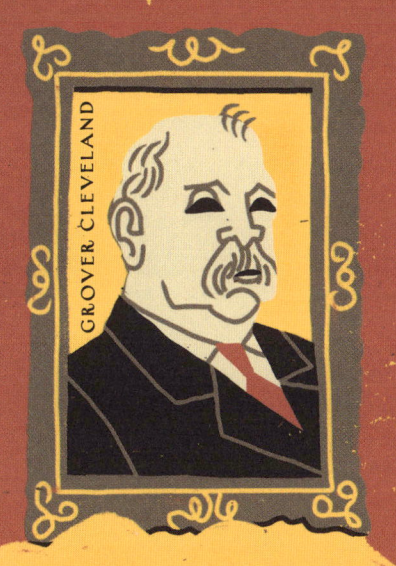

PRIVILEGE AND PERSEVERANCE

GROVER CLEVELAND

Philippa Bosanquet was born in Lincolnshire, England, in 1920. As the granddaughter of US President Grover Cleveland and daughter of a wealthy steel tycoon, hers was a life of luxury. But despite her riches, her early education was poor, partly because girls of her status were expected to marry into wealth – and that was something which didn't require formal schooling.

Nonetheless, she wanted to learn. With hard work and determination, she completed a Latin correspondence course where her lessons were done by post (long before online learning existed!). At Oxford University, she studied Philosophy, Politics and Economics and three years after obtaining her degree, she married fellow Oxford graduate Michael Foot. Though they eventually divorced, Foot kept and used her new surname across all her incredible achievements.

THE SOMERVILLE SET

While at Oxford, Foot studied at the renowned Somerville College and swiftly became part of a circle of friends and fellow philosophers who influenced each other's pioneering work. They shared their writings and thrashed out ideas, pushing each other to think about big questions – and not always agreeing.

During World War II, Foot's studies were paused when she served as an economist for the government in London. But after the war, she moved back to Somerville and focused only on philosophy. In 1969, Foot moved to the United States where, at several prestigious universities, she honed and nurtured her ideas. She focused on something called everyday ethics – that is, the moral decisions we make in our day-to-day lives.

What does being morally good look like?

Why strive to be morally good?

How do we judge moral 'goodness'?

How can we write about it?

ACTIONS AND THEIR CONSEQUENCES

One idea that Foot picked holes in was called consequentialism. This theory says that we should judge actions as good (moral), or bad (immoral), based on what happens as a result of the actions. For example, most people agree that stealing is bad. But if a person stole medicine to save someone's life, we might agree that the consequence justified the action and that, in this case, stealing is good.

But Foot was not convinced that this theory worked. Judging morality by looking at people's actions and the results as isolated events was, she said, too subjective. That meant an action could be good or bad solely based on people's beliefs or feelings. But who gets to decide? What would their reasoning be? Foot thought human actions were too complex to be judged this way.

POSITIVE AND NEGATIVE RIGHTS

Foot was faced with a problem. If we cannot judge our moral goodness by our actions and their consequences alone, then how can we judge it? And how can we apply it to our daily lives? One answer, she thought, is to look at our human rights. She divided these into two types: positive and negative.

A positive right is one that gives you (the rights holder) benefits. For example, you have the right to food, water, shelter, education, medical care, and so on. We have a duty to make sure others have these things too.

A negative right is one that allows things not to happen to you. You have the right to not be harmed, and we have a duty not to harm others.

When she looked at these rights, Foot wondered if it is ever morally right to act in a way that knowingly causes harm to others. Is there a difference between a person actively hurting someone and someone being hurt through a person's inaction? What do we do when a single act both benefits and harms at the same time? Puzzling through these big questions led Foot to come up with a series of thought experiments.

A LIFEGUARD'S DILEMMA

Think about the difference between these two scenarios:

RESCUE I

Imagine a lifeguard in a vehicle is patrolling a sandy bay. They see that one person is caught in the waves and so head out to rescue them. Before the lifeguard completes the rescue, they spot another five people further out who also need saving. To save the other five people, the lifeguard must abandon rescuing the first person. What should the lifeguard do?

RESCUE II

Imagine the same lifeguard from the first story sees five people who need saving from the water. To reach them in time, the lifeguard must drive the shortest route possible, but there is a sixth person who is in the way and will be killed if the lifeguard takes this route. What should the lifeguard do?

Foot said that most people will agree that it's acceptable for the lifeguard to save the five people in the first rescue, but not the second. This is because in Rescue I the lifeguard's inaction would let someone die, but in Rescue II the lifeguard's action would cause someone's death. In this case, the negative right not to be harmed is seen as more important than the positive right to be rescued.

THE TROLLEY PROBLEM

A trolley is an American term for a tram.

Foot went on to invent another problem to try to understand the moral difference between letting an event happen and interfering to stop it from happening. It's called the Trolley Problem.

Imagine a trolley without any brakes is charging along a track. There are five people up ahead who will die if it continues on its path. The driver can steer the trolley onto a different track, but there is one person on that track who will die if this action is taken.

If the driver does nothing and lets the tram follow its course, five people will die and the person on the other track will live. If the driver acts to steer the tram away, five people will be saved but the person on the other track will die. What should the driver do?

THE PRINCIPLE OF DOUBLE EFFECT

In the Trolley Problem, Foot insisted that it wasn't enough to think about the difference between acting to cause harm and letting harm happen by not acting. She urged us to think about something called the 'principle of double effect'. This idea tries to answer the question of whether an action is ever morally okay when the outcomes of the action are both good and bad.

Foot says that we can judge such an act to be morally acceptable if:

1. The action is not wrong in itself. (Example: The act of changing direction is not wrong.)
2. The outcome that is bad was not an intended consequence. (Example: The intention of changing direction is to save five people, not to kill one person.)
3. The good outcome didn't happen directly because of the bad outcome. (Example: Five people being saved is the result of the tram switching track, not because it went on to kill one person.)

Foot wanted us to apply this principle to decisions in our everyday lives because, she said, it would help us to make morally good choices.

A GIFT THAT KEEPS ON GIVING

Everyday goodness was at the heart of everything Foot did. She strived daily towards being just and being charitable and she was an early member and lifelong supporter of Oxfam, a charity based in her beloved Oxford. Impressively, she continued to write and talk about her ideas well into her eighties. She died on her 90th birthday, having gifted the world her cutting-edge ideas, curiosity and dedication to understanding what it means to be morally good.

Judith Jarvis Thomson (1929–2020)
An American moral philosopher who, among other things, expanded on Foot's thought experiment to inspire what became known as 'trolleyology'.

Ludwig Wittgenstein (1889–1951)
An Austrian-born philosopher whose writing on the logic and limits of language in expressing philosophical problems was a great influence on Foot.

Elizabeth Anscombe (1919–2001)
A committed Catholic philosopher from England who opposed consequentialism and favoured taking into account people's intentions when judging their behaviour.

AFRICAN PHILOSOPHY

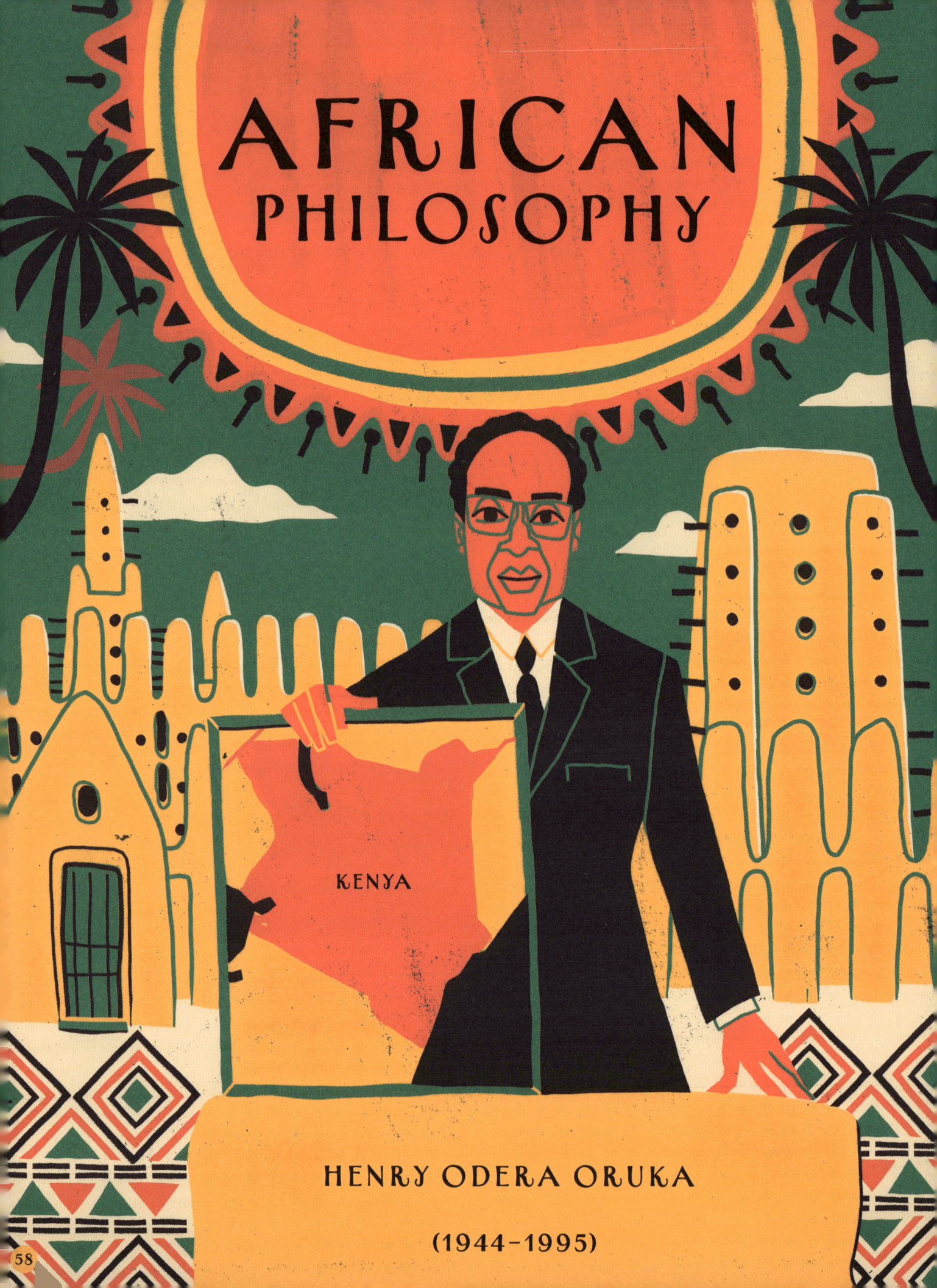

HENRY ODERA ORUKA

(1944–1995)

SCRAMBLING FOR AFRICA

In 1884, a group of leaders from wealthy European countries met for a conference in Berlin, Germany, to discuss trading boundaries in Africa. By the end, they had selfishly split up large parts of the continent for their respective countries to rule – all without the input of African people and leaders. The colonisation of African countries, or 'Scramble for Africa' as it was called, was a brutal and bloody process. Britain and France, as well as Belgium, Germany, Italy, Portugal and Spain, invaded huge territories of land, taking control and enforcing discriminatory laws on non-white people.

SIMPLIFYING AFRICAN WORLDVIEWS

European colonisers and Christian missionaries on journeys to convert people encountered many rich and varied cultures across Africa. But rather than working to understand and respect the detailed workings of these cultures and their interactions, the colonisers re-organised African people into new, drastically simplified groups. These were often based on a dominant language, sets of prominent physical features or geographic location. The colonisers also presented Africans as having simple, undeveloped worldviews, and they used this to justify their actions and ideas of superiority.

STUDYING FOR FREEDOM

Henry Odera Oruka was born in 1944 in Nyanza Province, Kenya, which at the time was a British colony. On completing school, he left his hometown to study Science and Philosophy at the University of Uppsala in Sweden. Afterwards, he was so captured by philosophy that he went to the United States to study even more! A key focus of Oruka's research was ideas of freedom. Through his work, Oruka, alongside many African people at home and abroad, fought for an end to colonialism.

AN INDEPENDENT WAY OF THINKING

Independence movements across Africa were fuelled by African intellectuals and theorists, many of whom had been to European or North American universities. Non-Africans claimed that these thinkers and their brilliant ideas were Western rather than African, and so belonged to the history of Western ideas. But Oruka challenged their narrow view of African ideas. When it came to philosophy, he argued that there was a long tradition of African thought that was not rooted in or dependent on Western influences.

IS THERE SUCH A THING AS AN AFRICAN PHILOSOPHY?

Oruka thought so! However, some philosophers disagreed, arguing that no significant work existed that could be called African philosophy. Others retorted, saying that even if that was the case, the decades of theorising and discussion that Oruka prompted around the idea of African philosophy was enough to show its existence. So then, what does African philosophy look like?

SAGE PHILOSOPHY

At the heart of Oruka's concept of African philosophy was the role of the sage. A sage is a person regarded by others in their society as wise and knowledgeable; a person others go to for personal guidance or for help with big questions about nature, reality, morality and the supernatural. In African society, Oruka said, there are two types of sage:

A FOLK SAGE

This person, often an elder, follows traditional customs and passes on sayings and lessons from previous generations. Oruka pointed to Ogotemmêli of the Dogon community in Mali. Ogotemmêli was a blind hunter, priest and wise man who shared traditional advice and stories about his community.

A PHILOSOPHIC SAGE

This person takes a critical, rational approach to knowledge, values and the world. Oruka's example was Paul Mbuya Akoko of the Luo people of Kenya. Mbuya was a paramount chief and spiritual leader who had great knowledge of the traditions and beliefs of the Luo. He used this knowledge to answer philosophical questions.

The main difference between the two sages is that the advice of a folk sage is rooted in their accepted local and traditional customs and beliefs, and the advice of a philosophic sage is based on their critical approach to ideas from inside and outside their community.

SOCRATES THE SAGE

Importantly, a sage is not a uniquely African role. Oruka said that a philosophic sage is simply a kind of philosopher. According to an ancient Greek thinker called Pythagoras, a philosopher is a 'lover of wisdom'. Oruka thought this was a good way to describe a sage. In his view, Socrates was a philosophic sage because his main role was guiding others towards a better society.

AUTHENTICALLY AFRICAN

Oruka argued that the philosophy practised by African philosophic sages was authentically African. This is because philosophic sages had existed across Africa long before colonialism, so they were not influenced by non-African education and philosophical traditions. Even more, Oruka believed that philosophic sages were vital to help reach solutions to the problems faced by postcolonial African societies.

SHOULD RICH COUNTRIES HELP POOR COUNTRIES?

Two of the biggest problems in postcolonial African countries were poverty and hunger. From the 1960s, discussions took place about whether the world's richest countries should help the world's poorest countries. After all, lots of the rich countries' wealth came from colonialism and exploitation such as slavery. Furthermore, when it came to environmental damage, rich countries were causing most of it and poor countries were suffering from the effects. Oruka began focusing his thought on global inequality and ethics, speaking out against something called the Lifeboat Theory.

THE LIFEBOAT THEORY

This was an argument against helping poor countries by giving foreign aid, put forward in 1974 by American ecologist Garrett Hardin. Hardin argued the world's richest countries were like safe, spacious lifeboats, and they should not share their wealth to help the world's poorest countries, which were unsafe, crowded lifeboats.

Sharing wealth would make poor countries poorer by weighing down their unsafe lifeboats. But letting people migrate to richer countries would weigh down the safe lifeboats, making them unsafe too.

SINKING THE LIFEBOAT THEORY

Well, Oruka thought this theory was nonsense. In his article called 'The Philosophy of Foreign Aid', he asked us not to think of helping other countries as a simple matter between imaginary boats. Instead, we can justify foreign aid because it is:

1. An act of charity.
2. A way to benefit global trade which helps everyone.
3. A way for rich countries to fix their historical wrongs.

Oruka explained his idea with a new metaphor showing the human population as a family sharing earth's resources.

People could easily relate to this framing of the issue: it was less abstract, more compassionate and placed the emphasis on our commonality and not our differences.

A POWERFUL VOICE

Oruka joined the University of Nairobi in 1970. There, he worked hard to build a department dedicated to philosophy and became its leading thinker. In fact, he was such a dominant voice that after his death in 1995, the department struggled to survive. Even so, thanks in part to the strong foundations he laid, African philosophy is now widely recognised and, indeed, thriving! Moreover, beliefs like Hardin's still persist, so it is vital to remember and continue Oruka's message of compassion.

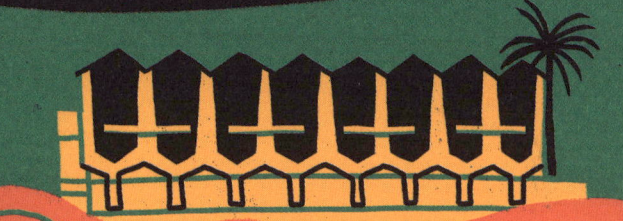

Dismas A. Masolo (1952–)
A Kenyan philosopher who worked with Oruka researching sage philosophy, focusing on French-speaking African countries.

Valentin-Yves Mudimbe (1941–)
Mudimbe is famous for *The Invention of Africa* in which he showed how colonialism created new myths about African pasts.

Nkiru Nzegwu (1954–)
A Nigerian philosopher, artist and art historian. Nzegwu fights against misrepresentation of African cultures and for women's voices to be heard across multiple disciplines.

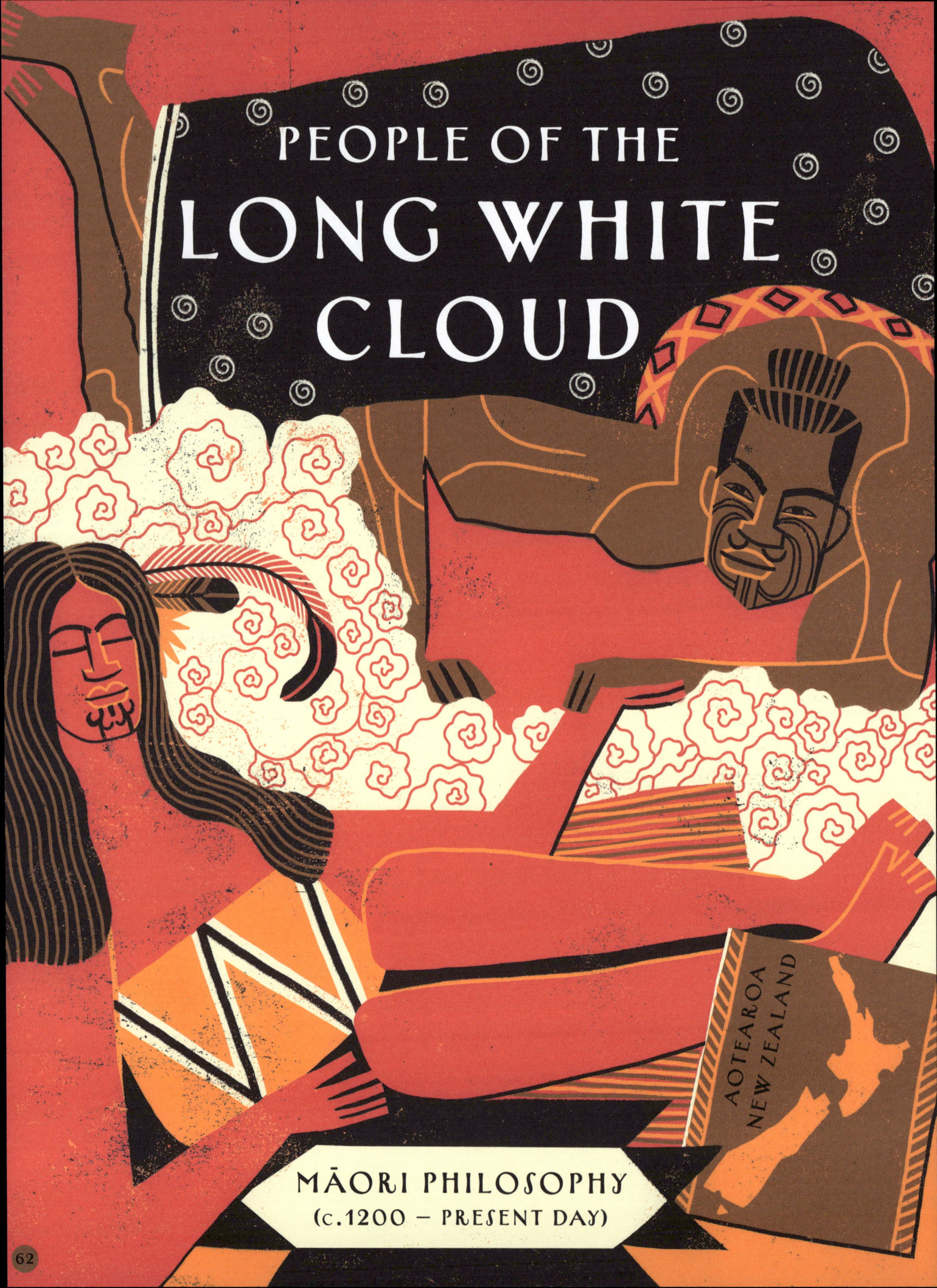

PEOPLE OF THE LONG WHITE CLOUD

MĀORI PHILOSOPHY
(c.1200 – PRESENT DAY)

THE PEOPLE OF THE CANOE

About 85 million years ago, a piece of land broke away from the ancient supercontinent Gondwanaland and drifted out across the southern sea. Cut off from other land masses, its unique animal and plant species evolved and flourished. Flightless birds roamed the undergrowth, from chicken-sized kiwis to moas taller than an ostrich. Dense forests climbed the mountains' steep sides and there were no mammals or large predators to be seen.

Then, around the 11th and 12th centuries, Polynesian explorers in ocean-going canoes spotted a long white cloud on the horizon. Sailing closer, the *tangata o te waka* – the people of the canoe – found a new, strange land and decided to make it their home. This was Aotearoa.

THE PEOPLE OF THE LAND

Over time, more canoes came to the islands. Different tribes settled on the coasts and spread inland along rivers into the forests and mountains. They adapted their ways to this new home and wove them into their stories, becoming *tangata whenua* – people of the land.

With the new people, however, came rats and dogs that the native animals had no defence against. The flightless birds were easy prey for hunters to feed their families, and within a few centuries, many had become extinct. The loss of the moa especially affected the new people, causing a shift in their view of their island homes. Then, one day, a different kind of canoe appeared on the horizon.

In 1642, a Dutch ship arrived, had a brief skirmish with the local people and left. They renamed the islands Staten Landt and then Nova Zeelandia (New Zealand in English).

The next European incursion wasn't until 1769, when James Cook, guided by the Tahitian navigator Tupaia, sailed around the coasts of the northern and southern islands. There was more violence, and more Māori were shot.

From around 1800, waves of British settlers came, keen to farm, cut timber and dig gold mines, which resulted in the destruction of the natural environment. With the addition of European weaponry, wars between the tribes worsened and violence between Māori and settlers increased.

MĀORI AND PĀKEHĀ

In Te reo, the Māori language, *māori* meant 'ordinary' or 'normal'. European settlers used the word to refer to all the islanders, but Māori didn't see themselves as a single group. Instead, they belonged to different independent tribes called *iwi*, and families called *hapū*. Māori called the European settlers Pākehā, meaning 'non-Māori New Zealander'.

A CULTURE UNDER ATTACK

Māori culture was being steadily eroded as part of the colonising process, and the Māori peoples became second-class citizens. But in the 20th century, the tide started to turn. Activists began the fight for Māori rights, traditional meeting houses were built and repaired, old stories were collected and retold, and new interest in Māori language, culture and philosophy grew.

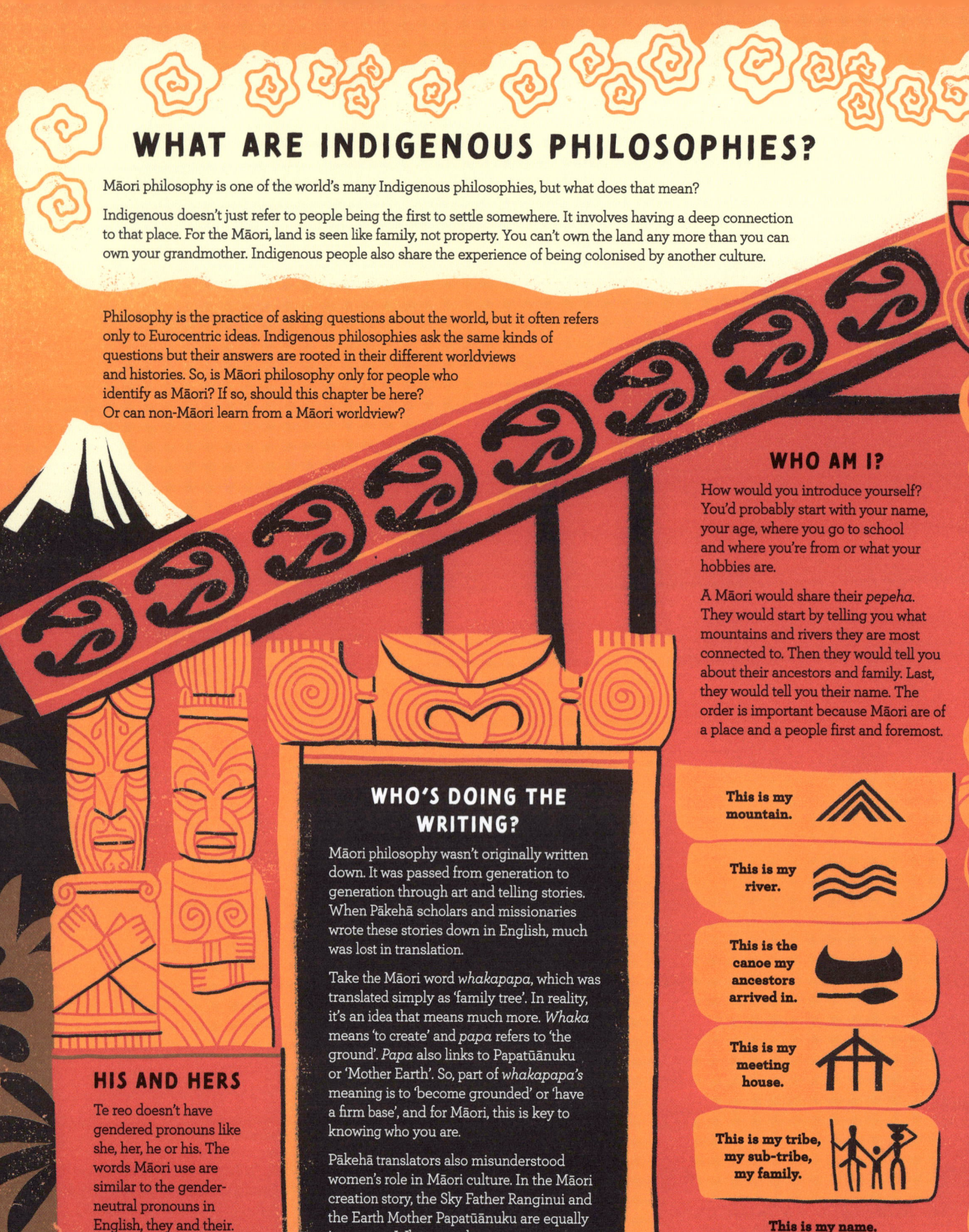

WHAT ARE INDIGENOUS PHILOSOPHIES?

Māori philosophy is one of the world's many Indigenous philosophies, but what does that mean?

Indigenous doesn't just refer to people being the first to settle somewhere. It involves having a deep connection to that place. For the Māori, land is seen like family, not property. You can't own the land any more than you can own your grandmother. Indigenous people also share the experience of being colonised by another culture.

Philosophy is the practice of asking questions about the world, but it often refers only to Eurocentric ideas. Indigenous philosophies ask the same kinds of questions but their answers are rooted in their different worldviews and histories. So, is Māori philosophy only for people who identify as Māori? If so, should this chapter be here? Or can non-Māori learn from a Māori worldview?

WHO AM I?

How would you introduce yourself? You'd probably start with your name, your age, where you go to school and where you're from or what your hobbies are.

A Māori would share their *pepeha*. They would start by telling you what mountains and rivers they are most connected to. Then they would tell you about their ancestors and family. Last, they would tell you their name. The order is important because Māori are of a place and a people first and foremost.

WHO'S DOING THE WRITING?

Māori philosophy wasn't originally written down. It was passed from generation to generation through art and telling stories. When Pākehā scholars and missionaries wrote these stories down in English, much was lost in translation.

Take the Māori word *whakapapa*, which was translated simply as 'family tree'. In reality, it's an idea that means much more. *Whaka* means 'to create' and *papa* refers to 'the ground'. *Papa* also links to Papatūānuku or 'Mother Earth'. So, part of *whakapapa's* meaning is to 'become grounded' or 'have a firm base', and for Māori, this is key to knowing who you are.

Pākehā translators also misunderstood women's role in Māori culture. In the Māori creation story, the Sky Father Ranginui and the Earth Mother Papatūānuku are equally important. When translators came across a story about Io, a different male creator, he seemed more familiar to their own Christian ideas. They decided this story was more important - and true - than the story involving Papatūānuku.

HIS AND HERS

Te reo doesn't have gendered pronouns like she, her, he or his. The words Māori use are similar to the gender-neutral pronouns in English, they and their.

This is my mountain.

This is my river.

This is the canoe my ancestors arrived in.

This is my meeting house.

This is my tribe, my sub-tribe, my family.

This is my name.

What would your *pepeha* be? If you don't live near mountains or rivers, think about places in nature that are meaningful to you.

WHAT IS A GOOD WAY TO ACT?

The pepeha *tells us that Māori see themselves in connection with the people – both past and present – who they are related to and the land they are anchored to.*

When it comes to ethics, or the right way to behave, Māori believe the decisions you make need to put the community rather than yourself first. And because the natural world is part of your community, that must be considered too.

WHAT IS TIME?

Imagine time is a line that stretches from the past to now and on into the future, and you are walking along it. Which way are you facing?

In a Western worldview, you'd be walking forwards, with the past behind you and the future ahead.

In a Māori worldview, you'd be walking backwards into the future while looking at the past. That's because you can see what has come before, but you can't see what is to come.

But what if time wasn't like a line at all? What if it was like a spiral? The tightly furled spiral of a fern or koru can be seen as a symbol of how the past and present are connected. In carvings on meeting houses, Māori family lines are sometimes shown as a double spiral with each generation represented by a notch. It's like the double helix shape of DNA, which also shows how our ancestors are present in us.

PROTECTING OUR ANCESTOR

Aotearoa means 'long white cloud', which the people of the canoe saw on the horizon all those years ago. Māori philosophy has evolved from the history of Aotearoa. As part of that philosophy, the islands and the whole world are seen as our ancestors which we, as part of their family, have a duty to protect. This view and other Māori insights on how to live can speak to us all, no matter where we're from.

Georgina Tuari Stewart (1961–)

(Ko Matauri te moana, ko Te Tāpui te marae, ko Ngāti Kura te hapū, ko Ngāpuhi-nui-tonu te iwi)

A philosopher and scientist who looks at the place of Māori thought in education.

Krushil Watene (1979–)

(Ngāti Manu, Te Hikutu, Ngāti Whātua Ōrākei, and the Pacific island of Tonga (Hunga, Vava'u))

A philosopher who is particularly interested in how a Māori perspective can help make the world a more just place.

Kiri Prentice (1980–)

(Ngāi Tūhoe, Ngāti Awa)

A Māori psychiatrist and YouTuber, creating videos to improve healthcare by uncovering and explaining Māori philosophy.

ANIMALS AND US

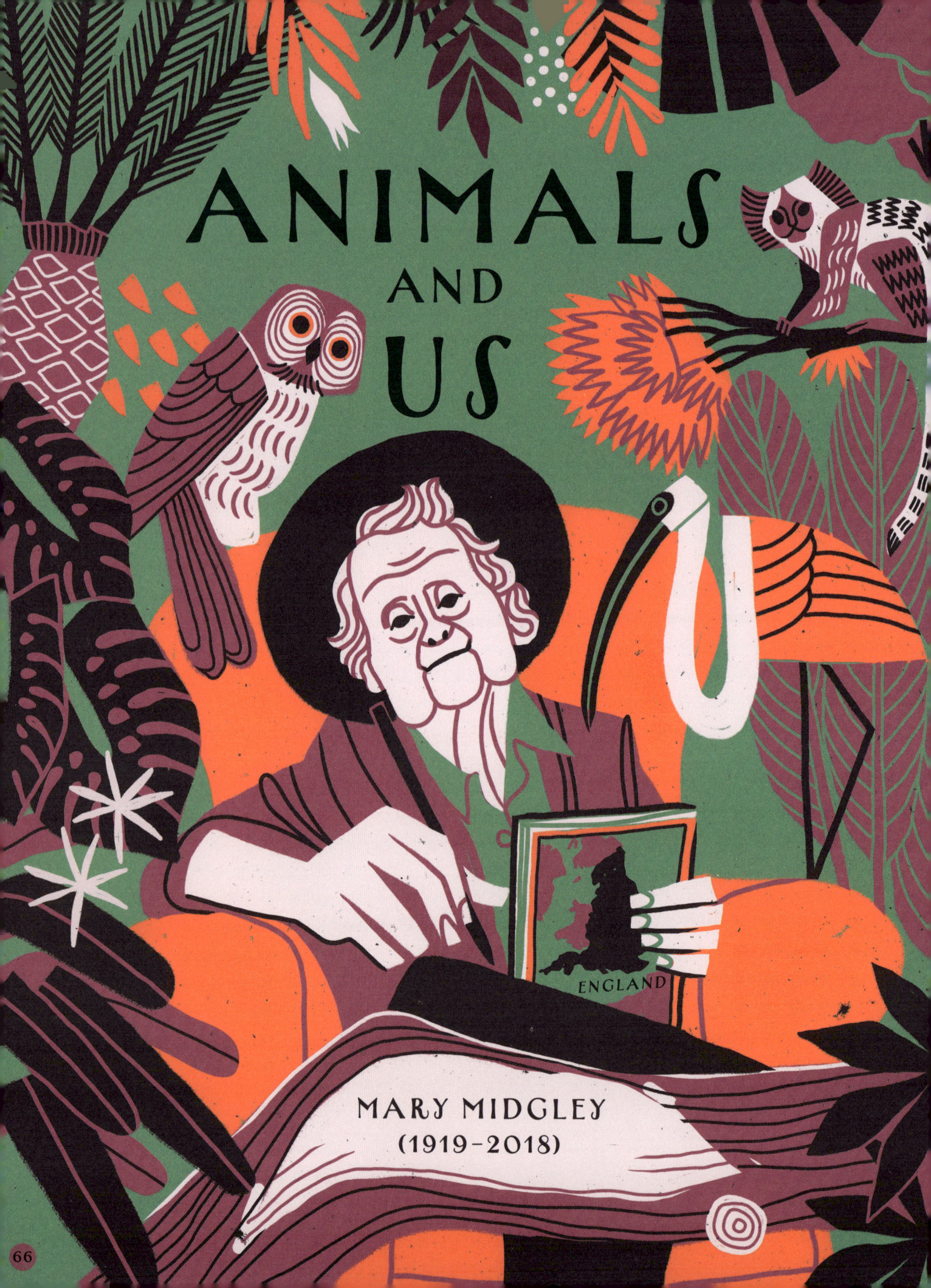

MARY MIDGLEY
(1919–2018)

ANIMALS AND US

Humans and animals have shared this planet for hundreds of thousands of years. During that time, we have eaten animals and been eaten by them, farmed them, hunted them for sport and invited them into our homes. We have seen animals as enemies, servants, the next meal and well-loved friends.

Over the years, philosophers have asked questions about our relationship with animals. What is the difference between animals and people? How should we treat animals? Do animals deserve to be treated morally? Do animals have value in themselves or are they only important if they're useful to us? These questions have led to some challenging answers about the place of animals in our world.

A BRIEF HISTORY

Being able to reason is the highest attribute. Animals can't reason. They are only there for humans to use.

Aristotle (384–322 BCE)

Also, animals don't have souls!

Thomas Aquinas (1225–1274 CE)

Language is the test of reasoning and animals don't have it. Really, they're just like machines.

René Descartes (1596–1650)

Without language, we can't form social contracts. Animals can't talk and that's an end to it.

Thomas Hobbes (1588–1679)

It's clear animals do have some simple mental abilities.

John Locke (1632–1704)

And they learn from experience.

David Hume (1711–1776)

Animals can't reason and so are only useful as far as humans have a use for them. But mistreating animals is wrong. It might lead to mistreating humans.

Immanuel Kant (1724–1804)

That's right - being cruel to animals sets a bad example for children.

Mary Wollstonecraft (1759–1797)

It isn't whether animals can reason or talk - the question is can they suffer?

Jeremy Bentham (1748–1832)

As a vet, I can tell you they do! Animals are sentient beings. They are conscious in a way that a rock or shovel are not.

William Youatt (1776–1847)

Utilitarianism means aiming for the greatest happiness and the least unhappiness in any situation – shouldn't that be true for animals too?

John Stuart Mill (1806–1873)

Animals have, like us, evolved to have feelings.

George John Romanes (1848–1894)

TIME FOR A RETHINK

Though groups had been questioning cruelty to animals since the early 19th century, in the 20th century there was a rapid increase in factory farming and animals being used in scientific experiments. TV and films also began to give us vivid pictures of wildlife and the ways they live. This caused a wider rethink about our relationships with the non-human inhabitants of the world, and one philosopher who took part in this reconsideration was Mary Midgley.

MARY MIDGLEY'S STORY

Mary Midgley was born as Mary Scrutton in London in 1919, just after the end of World War I. At school, she often got into trouble for being untidy and disorganised but even so, she managed to get into Oxford University at a time when women were still viewed with some suspicion. When World War II started in 1939, many men, including students and professors, went away to fight. This gave space for women to make their voices heard.

WOMEN SOLVING PROBLEMS

At the time, philosophy was focused on what Midgley called atomising: breaking an idea down into its smallest parts – sometimes even a word at a time – and then looking at each of these separately. Philosophers were interested in questions like 'what is reality?' rather than in more practical, everyday problems like 'how should we behave?'. Mary Midgley, along with her Somerville set companions Iris Murdoch, Elizabeth Anscombe and Philippa Foot, began to question this.

PHILOSOPHICAL PLUMBING

To Midgley, philosophy was a lot like plumbing. Beneath the surface of buildings, there are complicated but necessary things going on and the same is true for human lives. We don't often think about those things from day to day, but when they start to go wrong – when a pipe begins to smell, or an idea becomes out of date – it makes us uncomfortable.

When we find a problem, Midgley said we need to lift up the floorboards to see what is really there – what we have inherited from the plumbers and philosophers who came before. She believed that once we understand their work, we can start to unravel or unplug any broken parts and begin to replace them.

SMALL CHILDREN AND ANIMALS

One everyday thing that Midgley was always fascinated with was animals. As a child, she preferred stuffed animals to dolls, but as a grown-up, it wasn't only cuddly creatures that interested her. After marrying philosopher Geoffrey Midgley, she left her university work to raise their three sons and during this time, she was reading every book she could get her hands on about animal behaviour – from ants to dolphins to zebras.

As she read and observed, she noticed many similarities between small children and animals! When she returned to being a full-time philosopher in her 50s, she was more convinced than ever that philosophy needed to wrestle with everyday problems, and one of the smelly pipes we needed to investigate was our relationship with animals.

GAIA

In the 1960s, scientist James Lovelock was working for NASA, researching how we could detect life on other planets. He started by thinking about what a lifeless planet looks like and how that was different to Earth, and he came up with the idea of Gaia.

This idea describes our world as one interconnected living system, like the many that make up our bodies or plants. Midgley felt the Gaia theory as an imaginative way to rethink how we see the world and our place on it, including the way we see animals. It was the opposite of atomising – it looked at the small parts and also how they worked in the big picture – and Midgley felt it was essential to do both.

RETHINKING BARRIERS

When she was asked why animals matter, Midgley replied with another question: why do other people matter? Most philosophies would agree that humans have a duty towards other humans to treat them fairly. But in our history, barriers have been put up that exclude different people from fair treatment by saying that they are not really human. People such as women, those from different races and people with disabilities have been seen as separate – on the other side of a wall.

Midgley saw that there was a species barrier that decided that animals are also separate to us. This meant we didn't have any duty towards them. She traced this attitude to the philosophers of the past and urged us to rethink their ideas. By rethinking this barrier, we would see that animals are the group to which we belong. We are not separate from them or from the planet that we share – the intricately interconnected system that is Earth. What we do day to day and how we relate to other creatures and the world needs to be thought about properly. We need to know why we think the things we do, and we need to decide, when we know why, if we still agree. Our decisions matter.

A PHILOSOPHER TO HER LAST BREATH

Mary Midgley died at 99 years old, just a few weeks after her last book *What Is Philosophy For?* was published. Her answers to that question continue to place philosophy at the centre of our lives, helping us to understand how to relate to the world and the other animals in it. Philosophy for Mary Midgley was every bit as practical and important as plumbing.

Tom Regan (1938–2017)
An American animal rights pioneer who believed that non-human creatures had value in themselves, not just because of their usefulness to us.

Lynn Margulis (1938–2011)
An American biologist who worked with James Lovelock on the Gaia theory.

Gary Francione (1954–)
An American philosopher and lawyer who argued for the right of animals not to be considered property.

AN ACCIDENT AT THE CROSSROADS

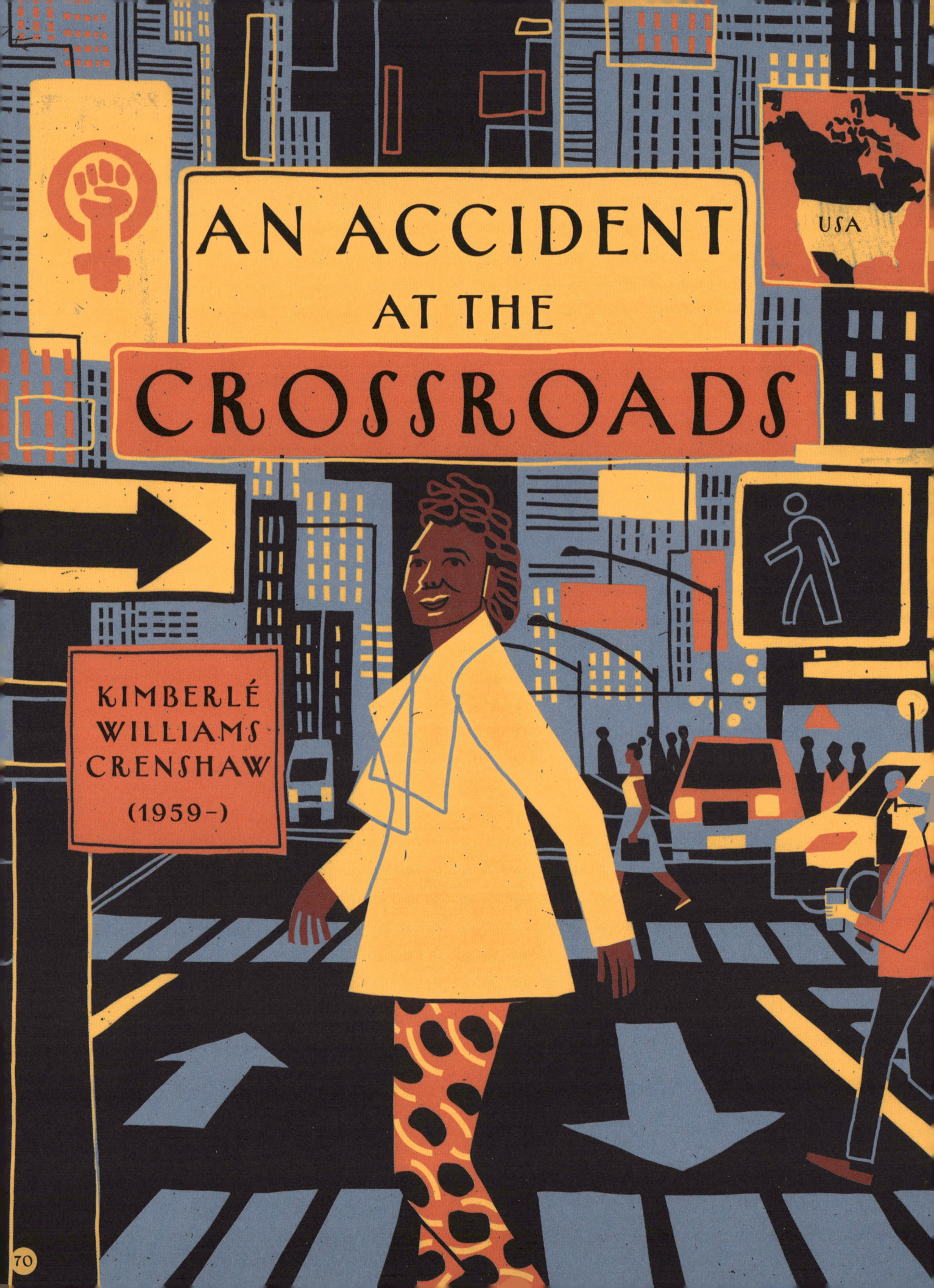

KIMBERLÉ WILLIAMS CRENSHAW (1959–)

A LONG HISTORY OF RACISM

← WHITE

COLORED →

Although slavery in the USA was formally abolished in 1865, former enslaved people – mostly of African heritage and particularly those living in the country's south – continued to be treated unfairly. Black people's rights were heavily restricted and housing and public facilities like schools, sports fields and libraries were segregated to prevent them from mixing with white people. The Ku Klux Klan, a group who believed white people were superior to all other races, committed violent crimes against Black people that were frequently overlooked by the courts.

YOUNG CRENSHAW

Kimberlé Williams Crenshaw was born in 1959 in Canton, Ohio, USA. In the classroom she excelled in debates and spelling bees, but her school years were not easy as she witnessed and experienced racism from her teachers and fellow pupils.

Crenshaw grew up during the height of the civil rights movement, and her parents, both teachers, were active in the fight for racial equality. They were a strong influence on Crenshaw, who aspired to be a lawyer to fight racial injustice.

THE CIVIL RIGHTS MOVEMENT

In the 1950s and 60s, people formed groups to campaign for racial equality in the law and society. They held protests, sit-ins and boycotts across the country, and these groups and their activities became known as the civil rights movement. Through their consistent collective action, the movement made many important breakthroughs such as the Civil Rights Act (1964), which outlawed discrimination, and the Voting Rights Act (1965), which removed barriers that prevented Black people from voting. But despite these incredible wins, racism in America did not end. Sadly, when the prominent leader and Baptist preacher Martin Luther King Jr was assassinated in 1968, the movement lost momentum.

GROUP THINKING

In the 1980s, Crenshaw studied at multiple universities including Cornell, Harvard Law School and the University of Wisconsin. At each one, she found that the idea of how gender related to race was not taught in any class. As someone who identified both as a woman and Black person, this puzzled her. She felt there was a clear link between her identities that needed to be discussed. In response, she and some fellow students formed a group to debate and develop ideas on race and society, called the Critical Race Theory Workshop.

How can we best understand race and racism?

How does racism in schools and workplaces lead to inequality in society?

Why are some people more vulnerable to discrimination than others?

How can naming a problem help to solve it?

CRITICAL RACE THEORY

One important theory the group developed was critical race theory. This idea says that race is socially constructed – that is, race and its meaning has been made up by humans and is not natural or biological.

In some societies, the idea of race has been used to falsely link people's natural physical traits, like skin colour, hair type and facial features, with imaginary ideas of how intelligent or kind or moral they are.

But crucially, saying that race is socially constructed doesn't mean that the effects of race and racism are not real. On the contrary, they have come to shape our society. Think of the way humans have created countries by drawing borders on a map – the countries and borders are made up, but in reality, they shape how we live.

COURT DISMISSED!

Another problem Crenshaw discovered while studying Law was the court case of Emma DeGraffenreid, an African American woman who unsuccessfully applied for a job at car manufacturing company in 1968. Years later, Emma sued the company, claiming she had been discriminated against as a Black woman. The company disagreed, saying they did not practise race or gender-based discrimination as they hired both Black people and women.

But the Black people they hired were all men and the women were all white. What's more, all these people were in low-level, low-paid positions. Finally, Emma was neither a Black man nor a white woman.

Ultimately, the judge decided Emma had not been a victim of double discrimination. According to the law, Emma's appeal to both race and gender was a 'super remedy' against unfair treatment and her case was thrown out of court.

AN ACCIDENT AT THE CROSSROADS

Crenshaw analysed Emma's case and created an analogy for thinking about this problem.

Imagine a busy crossroads where traffic is flowing in all directions. There is an accident in the middle at the intersection. Who caused the accident?

It is not always easy to identify which vehicle is to blame. It may have been caused by one or more than one vehicle, or even by the way the vehicles reacted to one another in these particular circumstances.

Now imagine the traffic is different forms of discrimination and a person standing at the intersection is harmed. Just like the vehicles, it's not easy to identify the particular form of discrimination that caused the harm. Crenshaw said that Emma was at the crossroads of two forms of discrimination.

NAMING, FRAMING AND SOLVING PROBLEMS

Linguistic philosophers look at how language helps us ask and solve questions about the ways we think and act, and Crenshaw's philosophy follows this idea. She said that only when we give a name to a problem, can we start to build a framework – a system of rules and ideas – to help solve it. In 1989, Crenshaw gave a name to Emma's problem: intersectionality. Intersectionality is when a person experiences multiple forms of discrimination that combine and compound in a single situation.

INTERSECTIONALITY BEYOND RACE AND GENDER

Besides gender and race, Crenshaw talked about other forms of identity, such as disability, age, class and sexual orientation, and encouraged us to see identities as relationships. How, she asked, do the identities you have relate to other people, human history, big ideas and the way society is organised?

Think about your age and what that allows you to do and not do. That feature of your identity has its own relationship with other people (like your parents or teacher), history (such as how children's rights have not always been recognised), structures in society (like child protection laws) and with ideas (like thinking about whether children should vote).

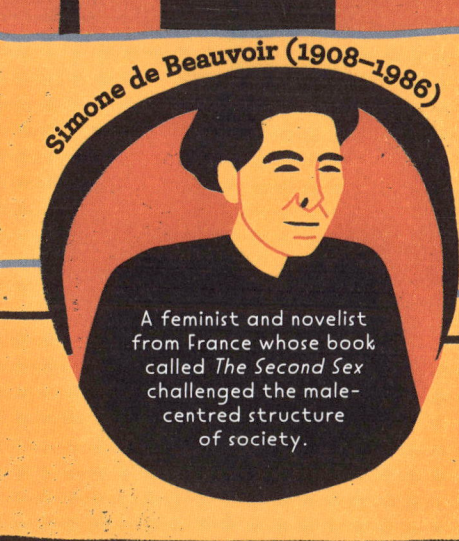

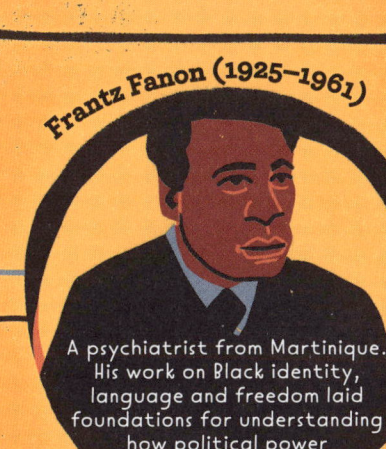

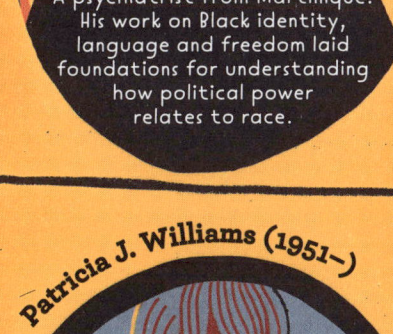

EACH CASE IS UNIQUE

When we look at the relationship between our identities and society, it's clear that some might give you privileges and others might be obstacles. Sometimes people are treated unfairly because of one of their identities, but they might be treated unfairly because of multiple identities. Since each person is different, each case will be different, which is why it's important to look at how identities intersect.

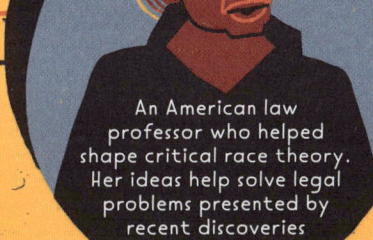

BRIGHTER, SAFER FUTURES

Today, Crenshaw is a pioneering law professor. Alongside teaching, she writes, gives speeches and advises on policies relating to gender and race around the world, guided by her thoughts on intersectionality. For Crenshaw, intersectionality goes beyond being a philosophical idea. It is part of a wider, ongoing project to fight racism, sexism and other forms of inequality in society.

Simone de Beauvoir (1908–1986)
A feminist and novelist from France whose book called *The Second Sex* challenged the male-centred structure of society.

Frantz Fanon (1925–1961)
A psychiatrist from Martinique. His work on Black identity, language and freedom laid foundations for understanding how political power relates to race.

Patricia J. Williams (1951–)
An American law professor who helped shape critical race theory. Her ideas help solve legal problems presented by recent discoveries in genetics.

GLOSSARY

Activist Someone who actively works to bring about political or social change.

Aesthetics The study of art and beauty.

Ascetics People who, often for religious or spiritual reasons, strictly deny themselves certain physical pleasures.

Autobiography The story of a person's life, written by that person.

Bible The holy book for Christians.

Boycott Choosing not to buy from a company or country as a protest.

Caliph The name that was given to leaders of the Islamic faith.

Civil disobedience Refusing to obey an unjust law or regulation in a peaceful manner.

Class Ways of dividing people in a society into higher or lower groups, based on things like wealth, education, jobs, race, the way they speak, or religion.

Colonialism When one power (usually a country) takes control of another territory and its people, usually by force.

Consequentialism The basic principle that we should judge our actions as moral or immoral based on their consequences alone.

Controversial Causing disagreement and argument.

Critical race theory This examines the way race and racism is built into our institutions, like our education system or the law.

Daoism (or Taoism) A Chinese philosophy based on ideas of 'harmony' and stemming from the writings of Lao Tzu.

Democracy In ancient Greece, this was a system of rule in which all citizens (the free men) participated in government.

Dialectic The art of discussion. In philosophy, the process of reasoning to reach an understanding of the truth beyond people's opinions.

Dialogue A conversation between two people.

Dictator A ruler with absolute control over a country which they maintain often using brutal methods.

Discrimination Treating people unfairly because of things like their skin colour, gender or sexual orientation.

Dynasty Periods of time under the rule of one family or clan.

Economist Someone who studies the way wealth (which includes money, the things we produce, the services we use) works in different societies.

Ethics The study of morality – that is, what is 'good' or 'bad', 'right' or 'wrong'.

Eurocentric Understanding the world only in terms of Western values and ideas, seeing these as superior to those of other countries or cultures.

Everyday ethics Applying moral meaning to decisions we make in our day-to-day lives.

Existentialism A branch of European twentieth-century philosophy exploring free will, rational thought and the place of the individual in the universe.

Exploitation Taking advantage of a person or group for your own benefit.

Foreign aid Help given by one country to another country. This could be in the form of money, food, equipment, training or personnel

Ge'ez The ancient language of Ethiopia.

Geometry A branch of mathematics relating to the distance, shape, size and position of points, lines, curves and surfaces.

Hierarchy A social hierarchy is a system of organising people in order of how important you think they are.

Incoherence Fuzzy thinking. Being unclear.

Intersectionality The ways in which different social categories that apply to a person (like class, gender, race) come together in their individual experience of discrimination

Jesuit A Roman Catholic order founded in 1540 that has been important in spreading different philosophical ideas. Jesuits travelled around the world to learn about other cultures in order to convert them to Christianity.

Logic The study of reasoning. Logic applies evidence and rational thinking to help us reach conclusions about what is true or false.

Manifesto A public statement of a person or group's aims, beliefs and intentions.

Metaphysics Enquiry into reality and existence that goes beyond asking questions that can be answered through science.

Objective When a position taken is based on evidence and fact rather than on opinions and personal feelings. The opposite of subjective.

For Susanne Langer, something that is objective exists in the outside world. We can experience it with our senses and describe it in words.

Ontology The study of the nature of being.

Oracle A person through whom a god or gods are believed to speak.

Phenomena Plural of 'phenomenon'. In science, a fact or event that we know exists because it can be observed.

Polymath Someone who is knowledgeable in many different areas. Throughout this book, you can find many famous philosophers who didn't only specialise in philosophy. This could be because philosophical questions relate to all aspects of life.

Presocratic philosophy The philosophy of ancient Greeks before Socrates's ideas and teachings.

Qur'an The holy book for Muslims.

Republic A country that is run by elected representatives rather than by a monarch.

Rights Something a person is entitled to. Human rights cannot be given or taken away by any person or government. Civil rights are rights that are granted and protected by laws in a person's own country.

Second-class citizen Someone whose rights and opportunities are considered less important than those of the dominant group in a society.

Subjective When something is based on feelings or beliefs or a specific point of view.

For Susanne Langer, something that is subjective exists inside our minds. We can share it with others using art.

Theology The study of religion.

Tolerance The ability to accept ideas or beliefs that are different from your own.

Torah The holy book for Jews.

Worldview How we see and understand the world. It affects the way we think, act and perceive other people.

ABOUT THE AUTHORS

JOAN HAIG

Joan Haig grew up in Zambia and Vanuatu and now lives in Scotland, where she is a lecturer and writer. In 2020 Joan edited *Stay at Home! Poems and Prose for Children Living in Lockdown*. Her debut novel, *Tiger Skin Rug*, was nominated for the Carnegie Medal. In 2022, she published *Talking History* – a book about history-making speeches – with Joan Lennon.

JOAN LENNON

Part Scottish, part Canadian, Joan Lennon is a novelist, poet and non-fiction writer, living in the Kingdom of Fife, Scotland, at the top of a tall house with a fine view of the River Tay. Her historical novels for 8-12-year-olds include *The Wickit Chronicles*, *The Slightly Jones Mysteries* and *Silver Skin*. In 2022, she published *Talking History* – a book about history-making speeches – with Joan Haig.